PS

 By the staff of Editions Berlitz

Preface

A new kind of travel guide for the jet age, Berlitz has packed all you need to know about Paris into this compact and colourful book, one of an extensive series on the world's top tourist areas.

Like our phrase books and dictionaries, this book fits your pocket—in both size and price. It also aims to fit your travel needs:

- It concentrates on your specific destination—Paris—not an entire country or continent.

- It combines easy reading with fast facts; what to see and do, where to shop, what to eat.

- An authoritative A-to-Z "blueprint" at the end of the book gives clear-cut answers to all your questions, from "Where do I get a bus to the airport?" to "How can I send a telegram?" plus tips on how to get there, when to go and planning your budget.

- Easy-to-read maps in full colour pinpoint sights you'll want to see.

In short, this handy guide will help you enjoy your visit to Paris. From the treasure-laden galleries of the Louvre to a boat ride on the Seine, from sipping an *apéro* on the Champs-Elysées to bargain hunting in the flea market, Berlitz tells you clearly and concisely what it's all about.

Let your travel agent help you choose a hotel.
Let a restaurant guide help you find a good place to eat.
But to decide "What should we do today?" travel with Berlitz.

Area specialist: Jack Altman
Photography: Loomis Dean; Erling Mandelmann (pages 2–3, 8, 10, 11, 36, 43, 45, 49, 54, 57, 65, 69, 73, 79, 92, 97)
We wish to thank Suzanne Patterson for her help with this guide, and we're also grateful to Ellen Stein, Mary Nicholson, the Office de Tourisme de Paris and the Office national français du Tourisme for their valuable assistance.

Contents

Maps: Paris p. 23, Western Paris p. 27, Louvre–Opéra p. 35, Montmartre p. 40, The Marais p. 41, Latin Quarter p. 51, Métro p. 128.

How to use this guide
If time is short, look for items to visit which are printed in bold type in this book, e.g. **Place Dauphine.** Those sights most highly recommended are not only given in bold type but also carry our traveller symbol, e.g. **Arc de Triomphe.**

Paris and the Parisians

The city and the people of Paris share a boundless self-confidence that exudes from every stone in its monuments and museums, bistros and boutiques, from every chestnut tree along its avenues and boulevards, from every little street-urchin, fashion model, butcher and baker, from every irate motorist and every charming maître d'hôtel. It is a self-confidence that will exhilarate anyone open to the breathless adventure of Paris, though it may intimidate people who dislike the light, movement and noise of life itself.

Some see it spilling over into arrogance—in the bombast of monumental architecture or in the overbearing attitudes of know-it-all street-philosophers. But looking around, you must admit they have something to be arrogant about. Stand on the Pont-Royal bridge in the late afternoon and gaze down the Seine to the glass-panelled Grand Palais, bathed in the pink-and-blue glow of the river's never tranquil waters. Already you sense that the light in this City of Light is of a very special kind, bringing phosphorescence to the most commonplace little square or side-street. In case the message is not clear, Paris offers unparalleled night-time illumination of its major historic buildings, avenues and squares, underscored by the ongoing battle between the city's monument-cleaners and automobile pollution.

Despite inevitable erosions of social change, Paris manages to sustain most of its myths and legends. Take the jargon of its topography, for example, names that evoke not just a place but a state of mind.

The Right Bank conjures up an image of bourgeois respectability. Historically the stronghold of merchants and royalty, it remains today the home of commerce and government. Faubourg Saint-Honoré offers the luxury of *haute couture* and jewellery shops and the authority of the president's palace (and the British embassy), while the Champs-Elysées claims the film, advertising and airline companies.

Hunting for bargains—whether in fashions, antiques, prints or stamps—is an absorbing Paris pastime.

The Left Bank on the other hand has always had a bohemian and intellectual image, dating back to the founding of the university and the monasteries. Today the Sorbonne, the Académie Française, the publishing houses and myriad bookshops continue to exert an intellectual magnetism. Left

Bank theatres typically prefer avant-garde drama to the *boulevard* comedy of the Right Bank.

The art galleries, doubtless needing the sustenance both of business and the intelligentsia, are about equally divided between Right and Left Banks, though the establishment-oriented galleries seem to be more in evidence on the Right Bank. The artists themselves remain characteristically on the periphery of both Right and Left Banks, in Montmartre and Montparnasse respectively.

A constant flow and interchange of citizenry from one bank to the other takes place over the 32 bridges of the Seine, a very accessible river well integrated into the town's life.

Paris is a city of people constantly on the move, at all hours of day and night—inevitable, really, since it's one of the most densely populated urban centres in the world. In nearly every one of Paris' 20 *arrondissements*, or districts, you will find shops, offices and apartments side by side and on top of each other, which makes the city's streets exceedingly lively. Don't be surprised if you become addicted to Paris' most marvellous sport—watching the world from a café table.

From that vantage point you can easily check on another of the town's legends—that of the good-looking women. The emphasis is not so much on "beautiful" or "pretty" but quite simply "good-looking". You may note that Parisian women are by and large *not* more or less pretty than elsewhere, but somehow they manage, with a colour combination, a hairstyle, a scarf tied in a particular way, but above all in the way they sit, stand or walk to just *look* good. Drawing on that communal self-confidence, they convince themselves—and nearly everybody else.

The key to the joy of just sitting and watching Paris go by is in the endless variety of the people. There is no "Parisian" type, physically speaking. The town's 2,600,000 population is drawn from every region in France—Brittany, Picardy, Alsace, Burgundy, Provence and Gascony—and the Parisian's traditional contempt for the "provinces" is matched only by his fierce regional loyalty to the distant home of his ancestors, most often just one generation removed.

Pigalle, with famed Moulin Rouge, lives on in round-the-clock whirl.

9

However dominant Paris may be in French art, literature, music, fashion, education, scientific research, commerce and politics, one area has been denied it—cuisine. There is no such thing as Parisian cuisine. This has the advantage, if you are a first-time visitor to France, of letting you come to the capital and sample each of the country's regional cuisines as you pick your way among the 11,000 or more bistros and restaurants around town. Often a region's representative restaurants cluster around the railroad station serving that area—like the Breton restaurants around the Gare

Montparnasse—for that is where yesterday's "provincials" stopped off and set up home as Parisians.

These "provincials" were drawn, like people the world over, to a city conceived and evolved on the grand scale but offering at the same time an intimacy on the neighbourhood level. While avenues and boulevards sweep up to

Paris scenes: elegant policeman orchestrates traffic outside Notre Dame; tourists try to bring the Louvre's masterpieces home on film.

monumental vistas, the narrow streets around the church of Saint-Séverin lead back to medieval times and the Rue de Varenne to the gracious classicism of the 18th century. In the same way, the Parisian has an imposing, sometimes forbidding reputation, but also wit, style and charm in his personal dealings that make him much more accessible than you would expect.

Paris has the astounding treasures of the Louvre and the ambitious new Beaubourg cultural centre. But it also offers those tiny storefronts on the Rue Jacob for collections of old artistic playing cards and Napoleonic tin soldiers. You can spend a small fortune on the most fabulous evening dress or buy the most stylish tee-shirt—for a thousand times less.

Don't expect to find any amazing bargains in the City of Light. Paris has been around long enough to learn the correct price for everything. The nightlife of the cabarets, theatres, opera, discotheques and nightclubs is *not* cheap, but it *is* still gay, and it is still an adventure. The real bargain is the magic of that light, movement and noise around the Paris streets. That costs just a little shoe-leather.

A Brief History

It all began in the middle of the river. Some Celtic fishermen and boatmen called Parisii set up their homes on an island in the Seine—the Ile de la Cité of today. The swiftly flowing waters provided good protection against invaders until the Romans conquered the town in 52 B.C. It was known as Lutetia or Lutèce, meaning marshland.

In Roman times the right bank of the river was too marshy to live on—so the town expanded to the Left Bank. Excavations have revealed the Roman arena, popular for the usual fights between gladiators, lions and Christians, and the public baths (see p. 71), dating from the 2nd and 3rd centuries A.D.

St. Denis brought Christianity to the city and was rewarded by decapitation on the hill of Montmartre. Legend and popular depictions of the event have Denis picking up his head and walking away with it.

Towards the end of the 3rd century Lutetia was overrun by barbarians, mostly Huns and Franks, and the town's inhabitants moved back to the fortified Ile de la Cité. Attila headed this way in 451 but the fervour of St. Geneviève's prayers is said to have persuaded him to spare the city. Clovis, King of the Franks, who showed good faith by converting to Christianity, arrived in 508 and settled down in the Palais de la Cité (now Palais de Justice). People moved back to the Left Bank and the church of Saint-Germain-des-Prés was built in the 6th century.

The Middle Ages

But Paris remained a backwater of the European scene until Hugues Capet established himself there in 987 and made Paris the economic and political capital of France for the Capetian dynasty. Under Louis VI (1108–37) Paris enjoyed its "agricultural age", when enclosed farms, *clos*, flourished. But the strength of Paris was its merchants who exploited the commerce of the Seine by collecting duties and taxes from ships passing through Paris, making the town rich under the motto: *Fluctuat nec mergitur* (It floats but it doesn't sink).

These revenues enabled Philippe Auguste (1180–1223) to construct Notre Dame cathedral, a fortress named the Louvre, aqueducts, fresh-water fountains and some paved streets. To protect his investment while away on the Third Crusade, he surrounded the growing city with walls.

Louis IX (1226–70) developed the spiritual and intellectual side of Paris life by building the Gothic masterpiece, the Sainte-Chapelle and many colleges on the Left Bank, including that of Robert de Sorbon (see p. 54). With a population of 100,000, Paris was the largest city in Western Christendom.

The mercantile backbone of the city proved itself in the 14th century when plague and the Hundred Years' War devasted France, leaving Paris at the mercy of the English. In 1356, with King Jean le Bon taken prisoner at Poitiers, the provost of the city merchants, Etienne Marcel, profited from the confusion and set up a municipal dictatorship. Though assassinated a year later, Marcel had showed that the Parisians themselves were a force to be reckoned with in France's history. The next king, Charles V, ever wary of Parisian militancy, built the Bastille fortress.

If the strife of the 14th century had been unsettling for Paris, that of the 15th was positively disastrous. In 1407, the Duke of Burgundy had the Duke of Orleans murdered on Rue Barbette, which led to 12 years of strife between the Bur- **13** gundians and Armagnacs. The carnage ended only with the capture of Paris by the English in 1420. Ten years later Joan of Arc tried and failed to liberate the town. The next year came the ultimate humiliation with the crowning of the young English King Henry VI at Notre Dame as King of France. In case that was not enough, the plague of 1466 felled thousands of Parisians.

Paris Takes Shape

Nonetheless the city remained resilient. With François Ier (1515–47), Paris learned to thrive under an absolutist and absentee monarch, busy with wars in Italy and even a year's imprisonment in Spain. The arts, sciences and literature flourished. Much of the Louvre was torn down and rebuilt along its present lines. A new Hôtel de Ville (town hall) was begun, as well as the superb Saint-Eustache church. The Parisians were already assuming that distinctive pride over the uniqueness of their town. Poet Pierre de Ronsard saw Paris as "the city imbued with the discipline and glory of the Muses".

The religious wars wreaked havoc and mayhem in Paris, starting in 1572 with the Massacre of St. Bartholomew—

3,000 Protestants were killed—and culminating in the siege of the city by Henri de Navarre in 1589. Before the Catholic League capitulated, 13,000 Parisians had died of starvation. Henri was crowned at Chartres and finally entered the city in 1594—but not before he had turned Catholic. His famous words, "Paris is well worth a mass", have remained an ambiguous comment on the merely political value attached to religion and the special

14

desirability of the French capital. Paris' myth was growing.

Henri IV did Paris proud once he was its master. He built the beautiful Place des Vosges and Place Dauphine, embellished the river banks with the Quais de l'Arsenal, de l'Horloge and des Orfèvres and constructed the Samaritaine hydraulic machine that pumped fresh water to Right Bank households till 1813. By far the most popular of France's monarchs, Henri IV was a notorious ladies' man and was known to his subjects as the Vert Galant. He completed the Pont-Neuf (despite its name, the city's oldest standing bridge) and the adjacent gardens, where he had been known to dally with his ladies.

The Conciergerie was the last stop for many on their way to the guillotine.

Young lovers carry on the tradition there today.

Under Louis XIII (1610–43), Paris began to take on the "fashionable" aspect that has become its mark. The Cours-la-Reine, precursor of the Champs-Elysées, was built for Henri's widow Marie de Médicis. Elegant houses went up along the Faubourg Saint-Honoré and tree-lined boulevards stretched clear across the city over to the Bastille, creating the airy sweep of modern Paris. The capital also consolidated its position as the hub of the country—with the establishment of the royal printing press, Cardinal Richelieu's Académie Française and other scientific institutions, such as the botanical gardens, and Paris' new ecclesiastical status as an archbishopric. The cardinal also deserves credit for the splendid Palais-Royal. With the Ile Saint-Louis—formed from two separate islands in 1614 by engineer Christophe Marie—and the residential development of the Marais and Saint-Germain-des-Prés districts, Paris was becoming an increasingly attractive place for nobles from the provinces.

Too much so for the liking of Louis XIV (1643–1715). To bring his overly powerful and independent aristocrats back into line he decided to move the court to Versailles, where palace life was ruinously expensive.

Paris continued to flourish with the landscaping (by Louis' counsellor Jean-Baptiste Colbert) of the Tuileries Gardens, the Champs-Elysées, the construction of the Louvre's great colonnade, the triumphal arches of Saint-Antoine, Saint-Denis and Saint-Martin and the Invalides hospital for soldiers wounded in Louis' wars. The Sun King's fears about Parisian talent for trouble-making led to the innovation of street-lighting (on moonless nights only). The city now numbered 560,000 inhabitants, almost six times as many as in the 13th century under Louis IX.

Paris asserted its cultural ascendancy in Europe with the organization of the academies of the arts, literature and sciences and the founding of the Comédie Française (1680) and other theatres under Louis XV. Cafés sprang up around the Palais-Royal, and the boulevard life was the animated focus of European intellectual ferment as the Revolution approached.

One of the last constructions of the Ancien Régime, begun in

1784, was a new wall around the city. This became a major factor in the revolutionary unrest, for it was there that the *fermiers-généraux* (financiers) collected taxes from merchants and artisans coming to do business in Paris.

Revolution and Empire

The Revolution of 1789 was more notable for its destruction than for additions to Parisian landmarks—though the removal of the Bastille and the monasteries and convents did create more open spaces. The Revolutionaries made special use of the stronghold of the Capetian dynasty: the Conciergerie in the Palais de Justice, the heart of the medieval kings' palace, became a prison for those condemned by Revolutionary tribunals. And Dr Joseph Guillotin, a member of parliament, who said the times demanded something more humane than the Ancien Régime's hanging, drawing and quartering, developed a new gadget to chop heads off.

With the advent of Napoleon, the city's development resumed. The emperor's frequent absences on foreign business did not hinder his projects for making Paris the capital of Europe. Detailed maps of the city and architectural plans for new buildings were always part of his baggage. Typically he found time during his stop-over in Moscow to work on the reorganization of the Comédie Française back home. While most visitors see Napoleon's mark in spectacular monuments—the Arc de Triomphe, the 12 avenues of the Etoile, the column of the Grande Armée on Place Vendôme—the emperor himself regarded his most important achievements as those more appropriate to a mayor than a world conqueror: increased supplies of fresh water for the city, the new food-markets, the five slaughter houses and the wine-market. His streamlined municipal administration and police force became a model for modern European urban government.

The centralization of power in the capital also made Paris a potential threat to the government—the concentration of aggressively ambitious bourgeois, dissatisfied workers and an intellectual class eager to try out its radical ideas. Typically the Revolution of 1830 came from an alliance of liberal bourgeois Parisian intellectuals, denied the right to publish their newspapers, and the printing-workers thrown into unemployment by the closing of **17** the papers. The 1848 Revolution which ended Louis-Philippe's "bourgeois" monarchy also originated in Paris when the government tried to forbid banquets held in the capital in support of electoral and parliamentary reform. Building Paris up as a great, lively, volatile capital of cultural, social and political innovation automatically turned it into a hotbed of trouble for its rulers.

Modernizing the City

Napoleon III, the great one's nephew, was literally scared into modernizing Paris. He had seen the popular uprisings of 1830 and 1848 flare up in the capital's densely populated working-class neighbourhoods around the city centre and wanted to prevent a recurrence. He commissioned Baron Georges Haussmann to do away with the clusters of narrow streets and alleyways that nurtured discontent and barricades. The baron razed them and moved the occupants out to the suburbs, creating the "red belt" which makes Paris one of the few Western capitals whose suburbia is not predominantly conservative.

The city was opened up by wide boulevards and avenues, giving Paris its modern airy look and highlighting the city's monumental churches and other public buildings. Furthermore, as the baron explained to his emperor, these avenues gave the artillery a clear line of fire in case of revolt.

But this Second Empire was also a time of gaiety and boisterous expansion, emphasized by world fairs in 1855 and 1867, attracting royalty from England, Austria, Russia and Prussia to look at the sparkling new city of Offenbach's operettas and the comedies of Labiche. This was the beginning of "gay Paree".

Then came war, the Franco-Prussian War, with a crippling siege of Paris in 1870 and another uprising, barricades and all. The Paris Commune —self-government of the workers—lasted 10 weeks (March 18 to May 29, 1871), until Adolphe Thiers, first president of the Third Republic, sent in troops from Versailles to crush the revolt.

Into the 20th Century

The Third Republic brought unparalleled prosperity to Paris. Projects begun under

La Belle Epoque—when you could hear Bruant sing at the Chat Noir.

Napoleon III, such as the new opera house and the gigantic Halles market (today moved out to the suburbs) were completed in the construction boom that followed the capital's triumphant resurrection after its defeat by the Prussians. By the 1890s Paris had risen to the fore as a cultural magnet.

Artists, writers and revolutionaries flocked to this hub of creative activity. Picasso arrived from Barcelona in 1900, followed by Modigliani from Livorno, Soutine from Minsk, Stravinsky from St. Petersburg, Gertrude Stein from San Francisco, and then the long stream of American writers and artists led by Ernest Hemingway and F. Scott Fitzgerald. Paris was Mecca, the myth so powerful that detractors of the Belle Epoque and the Gay Twenties were drowned out by the true believers raising another glass at La Coupole *brasserie* and dancing another foxtrot at Maxim's.

Two wars, of course, took their toll. Though the Germans did not make it to Paris during the First World War, they occupied the city for four drab years (June 1940 to August 1944) in the Second. It took Paris some time to recover. Typically, what the French remember best was the august parade of General de Gaulle and his fellow Resistance fighters down the Champs-Elysées; the expatriates' fondest memory, on the other hand, is of Ernest Hemingway "liberating" the bar of the Ritz Hotel. While much of the cultural magnetism had moved from Paris to New York, the French capital retained some of its mythic character with Jean-Paul Sartre holding existentialist court on the Left Bank and Juliette Gréco singing all in black in the jazz-cellars of Saint-Germain-des-Prés.

In May 1968, the students made the Latin Quarter a battle-ground against de Gaulle's Fifth Republic, another reminder of Paris' revolutionary capacity. Just as resolutely de Gaulle's successor Georges Pompidou asserted the strength of the city's bourgeoisie with the construction of new expressways along the Seine ("the city must adjust to the automobile") and la Défense complex of skyscrapers, "Little Manhattan", west of the Arc de Triomphe. Pompidou's crowning monument came posthumously with the Beaubourg Cultural Centre built under his inspiration to encourage a revival of the arts. The furore of enthusiasm and hostility for the revolutionary architecture of Beaubourg is testimony, 2,000 years after the Romans, that Paris is still a town worth fighting for.

On July 14th, France's veterans and Resistance fighters turn out.

What to See

The Seine

The river is by far the best place to begin to take the measure of Paris. Its mixture of grandeur and intimacy is the very essence of the city.

Stand on the Right Bank by the Pont Mirabeau, facing east. Upriver you'll see the Statue of Liberty (a scale-model of the New York original) on the next bridge, framed against the Eiffel Tower over on the Left Bank. This visual melding of the Old and New Worlds pre-pares you well for the cosmo-politan experience of Paris.

Again and again the Seine provides a spectacular van-tage-point for the city's great landmarks. The Eiffel Tower itself, the Palais de Chaillot and Trocadéro Gardens, the Grand and Petit Palais, the Palais-Bourbon, Louvre Museum and Notre Dame all take on a more enchanting, even dream-like quality if you see them first when floating by in a boat. This is of course even more true of the river's bridges, many of them also monuments to the capital's history.

For that all-important first impression, a **guided boat-trip** on the Seine is unbeatable (see page 26). But this also remains a river to be walked along, despite the encroachments of cars on rapid *voies express* along the banks. You can take delightful strolls right down by the river between the Pont Sully at the eastern end of the Ile Saint-Louis and the Pont de la Concorde and around the two river-islands. Nothing is more restful—and the ex-citement of Paris demands an occasional rest—than an hour on a bench beneath the poplars and plane trees along the Seine, especially early morning and late afternoon when that pink Paris light is at its best.

Getting your Bearings
Your orientation in Paris on foot or by car will be simplified by reference to five easily vis-ible landmarks—the Arc de Triomphe and Church of the Sacré-Cœur on the Right Bank; the Eiffel Tower and (jarring but nonetheless con-veniently visible) Tour Maine-Montparnasse skyscraper on the Left Bank; and Notre Dame Cathedral in the middle of the Ile de la Cité. Whenever you get lost, you should nor-mally not have to go more than a couple of hundred yards be-fore sighting one of these monuments on the horizon.

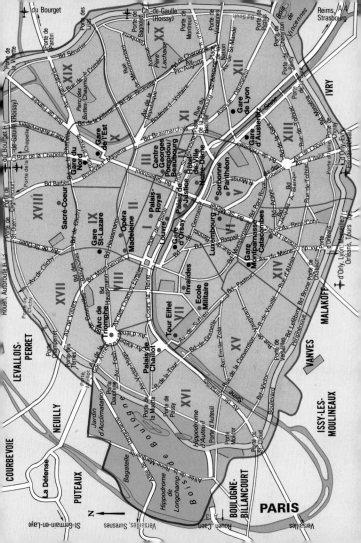

If you want to see the river from its bridges, there are four especially worthy of your attention. The **Pont-Neuf,** completed by Henri IV in 1607, was the first one built without houses: Parisians were pleased to walk across and see their river. It soon became a favourite spot for promenades, for street-

Old prints, magazines and books line stalls on the quais *of the Seine.*

singers, charlatans, amateur dentists, professional ladies, pickpockets and above all for the *bouquinistes* selling their old books and pamphlets out of boxes. Established booksellers on the Ile de la Cité were enraged and drove them off to the banks of the Seine, where they have remained ever since.

The **Pont-Royal,** built for Louis XIV in 1685, commands a splendid panorama of the Tuileries Gardens and the Louvre. It is the capital's most central bridge in the sense that it offers good views of the Grand and Petit Palais of the *grand-bourgeois* and the Ecole des Beaux-Arts and Académie Française of the intellectual community.

The **Pont de la Concorde,** truly the bridge of the French Revolution, went up between 1787 and 1790. Its support structure used stones from the demolished Bastille prison—especially galling for Royalists in that it was originally Pont Louis XVI. The name was duly changed to Pont de la Révolution the year before Louis was guillotined a couple of hundred yards from the bridge on the Place de la Concorde.

The **Pont Alexandre III,** distinguished architecturally by its single steel arch, represents the final flowering of that bumptiously proud 19th-century industrial spirit exemplified by the Eiffel Tower. The purists find its statues to Fame and Pegasus insufferably bombastic but lovers view them as an appropriately melodramatic touch to a moonlit stroll beneath the bridge's Belle Epoque lanterns.

Paris by Boat

You can see Paris by the river and hear multi-lingual commentaries on all the landmarks:

The Bateaux-Mouches, the largest, have open-air or covered seating according to the weather. They are the only ones offering lunch and dinner and a concert at 10.30 a.m. on Sundays (except for January and February). The regular 75-minute tour (10 a.m. to 10.30 p.m.) starts from the Quai de la Conférence by the Pont de l'Alma bridge going west to the Pont Mirabeau and turning back upriver to the Pont Sully at the far end of the Ile Saint-Louis and Ile de la Cité. The lunch (1 p.m.) and dinner cruises (8.30 p.m., ties obligatory, no anoraks and blue jeans) are more leisurely. Telephone 225-9610.

The *vedette* or motorboat tours take 60 minutes. Vedettes Paris Tour-Eiffel start by the Eiffel Tower at the Port de la Bourdonnais, 9.30 a.m. to 6 p.m. (9 p.m. Saturdays) going west to the Pont Bir-Hakeim and east to the Pont Sully and back (tel. 561-4645). Vedettes du Pont-Neuf leave from the Pont-Neuf bridge, Square Vert-Galant, 10.30 a.m. to 5.30 p.m. (9 p.m. Saturdays) to the Eiffel Tower and back around the islands (tel. 633-9838).

Right Bank
(Rive Droite)

L'Etoile–Concorde–Palais-Royal

Any tour of the Right Bank should begin at the **Place de l'Etoile** (officially, Place Charles-de-Gaulle), preferably on top of the **Arc de Triomphe.** One reason for climbing up Napoleon's gigantic triumphal arch (164 feet high, 148 feet wide) is to get a good view of the 12-pointed star, formed by 12 avenues radiating from the arch in a tour-de-force of geometric planning. The *place*, a vast sloping mound, cannot really be taken in at ground-level. The monumental ensemble, conceived by Napoleon as a tribute to France's military glories and heroes, was completed by Baron Haussmann. Over the years the arch has taken on a mythic quality as succeeding régimes have invested it with the spirit of the nation, republican or imperial.

Napoleon himself saw only a life-size wooden and canvas model. Louis-Philippe inaugurated the final version in 1836, complete with bas-reliefs and statuary celebrating the Republic's victories. It became the traditional focus for state

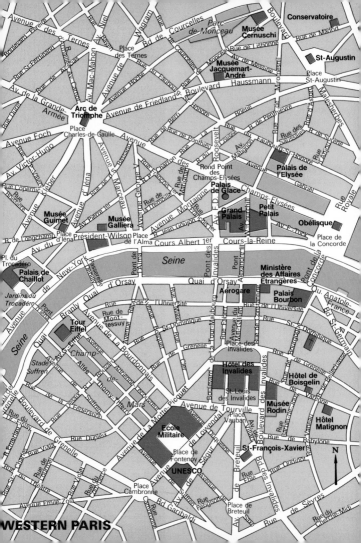

WESTERN PARIS

funerals of national political, military and even literary heroes—Victor Hugo was given a positively pharaonic tribute here after his death in 1885. In 1920, the Unknown Soldier—killed in World War I—was buried at the arch and three years later, the Eternal Flame was lit.

When Hitler came to Paris as a conqueror in 1940, this was the first thing he wanted to see; and, of course, General de Gaulle's triumphant march of Liberation in 1944 started from here.

Avenue Foch, leading away from Etoile, is the most majestic of the city's residential avenues and the best of the Baron Haussmann's grandiose conceptions. The **Champs-Elysées,** despite extensive commercialization, still deserves the title of the world's most-celebrated avenue. It stretches in an absolutely straight line from the Arc de Triomphe to the Place de la Concorde, lined with chestnut-trees all the way. The first two-thirds, as you walk down, are devoted to cinemas, shops and café terraces; you'll find the best people-watching

Driving round the Place de la Concorde is one of life's great adventures, especially at rush-hours.

28

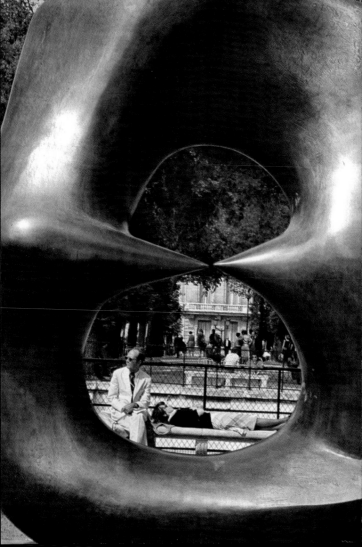

points at the corner of the Avenue George-V on the "shady" side and at Rue du Colisée on the "sunny" side. After the Rond-Point, a pleasant park takes you down to the Place de la Concorde. An interesting theory about the special appeal of the Champs-Elysées is that people look more relaxed and attractive when walking downhill—so ignore the ones going in the other direction.

The **Place de la Concorde** has had a hard time earning its name. More than 1,000 people were guillotined here during the Revolution, the drums rolling to drown out any incendiary words the condemned might utter. In 1934, bloody rioting against the government took place here. Ten years later it was the Germans' last hold in Paris. Today, with floodlit fountains and elegant lamps it is a night-time romance and a daytime adventure, both for the pedestrian pausing to enjoy the vast opening of the Paris sky and for the driver daring to make his way around it. (Along with the Etoile, it ranks as one of Europe's greatest challenges to the motorist's ability to survive, the centrifugal force flinging him out, he hopes, to his destination.) Smack in the centre you'll see Paris' oldest monument, the 75-foot pink syenite-granite obelisk of Luxor from the temple of Ramses II, dating back to 1300 B.C. For a change it's not something Napoleon brought back from his campaigns but a gift from Mohammed Ali, the Viceroy of Egypt, erected in 1836.

After the bustle of the Champs-Elysées and the Place de la Concorde, you'll appreciate the cool, peaceful park, the **Jardin des Tuileries,** named after 13th-century tile works. Their spaciousness is due in large part to the destruction of the Palais des Tuileries during the 1871 Commune (fragments can still be seen by the Jeu de Paume museum in the northwest corner). Children will enjoy the circular ponds on which boats are sailed and sunk almost all year round and the marionnette shows in spring and summer.

At the eastern end of the Tuileries stands the **Arc de Triomphe du Carrousel,** built about the same time as the more famous Arc de Triomphe. From this point you can look straight ahead to the Luxor Obelisk and Etoile's arch, a perfect illustration of the

Art moves outdoors: Henry Moore exhibit in the Tuileries Gardens.

lengths the French will go to achieve an effect—and only a spoilsport would complain. Unfortunately in recent years the view *has* been a little spoiled by the modern skyscrapers of la Défense beyond Etoile, but a little poetic imagination blots them out.

Leaving the Louvre Museum for a separate visit (see p. 66), cross the Rue de Rivoli to the **Palais-Royal.** There are few pleasanter places to dip back into the history of Paris. Completed in 1639 for the Cardinal Richelieu (after whom it was originally named the Palais-Cardinal), this serene arcaded palace with its garden of lime and beech trees and a pond where the young Louis XIV nearly drowned has always been a colourful centre of more or less respectable activity. In the days of Philippe d'Orléans, Regent of France during Louis XV's minority, the Palais-Royal was the scene of notorious orgies. The family's extravagance made it necessary to meet debts by turning ground-floor rooms into boutiques—the last of which still sell old coins, medals, engravings and an-

tiques—and cafés that attracted a fashionable society.

But in Paris the "beau monde" and "demi-monde" have always lived off each other and the Palais-Royal soon took over from the Pont-Neuf as the meeting-place of artists, intellectuals, charlatans, prostitutes and pick-pockets. On July 13,

Peaceful area around the Palais Royal recalls a more elegant age.

J. Klein, Lausanne

1789, a young firebrand orator, Camille Desmoulins, stood on a table at the Palais-Royal's Café de Foy and made the call to arms that set off the French Revolution the next day. At the other end of that era, Prussian General Blücher came to the Palais-Royal after Waterloo to squander 1,500,000 francs in one night at one of the many rambunctious gambling dens. Things are quieter now. Mothers and nannies wheel their babies in prams in the garden and the palace houses the High Court and the Ministry of Culture.

Once the scene of Paris' bustling, boisterous, odoriferous

food markets, **Les Halles** is now a district in the process of transformation. If for no other reason, it's worth going there to see the beautiful hybrid church of **Saint-Eustache.** This Gothic edifice built at the end of the Renaissance was patterned after Notre Dame. The funerals of Molière and La Fontaine took place here. Don't miss the remarkable stained-glass windows crafted according to medieval tradition,

Place Vendôme– Opéra–Madeleine

It's hard to find a more elegant place to work in than the **Place Vendôme,** an airy gracious octagon designed to provide an imposing setting for a statue of Louis XIV. Only his financiers could afford the rents here and nearly 300 years later the situation has not changed much: there are 19 banks (as well as world-famous jewellers, the Ministry of Justice and the Ritz Hotel) encircling the column with which Napoleon replaced the Sun King. The spiral of bronze bas-reliefs depicting scenes from the Great Battles, topped by a statue of Napoleon himself, was cast from 1,250 cannons captured from the Austrians and Russians at Austerlitz.

A quick walk up the Rue de la Paix—a slow one might prove ruinous to your budget —takes you past jewellers, goldsmiths and furriers to the **Opéra,** the massive epitome of the pretensions of Napoleon III's Second Empire. Started at the height of his power in 1862 (by architect Charles Garnier), when Paris claimed to be Europe's most glamorous capital, the Opéra was not completed until 1875. Its mixture of neo-classical styles is less of an aesthetic joy than a splendid act of conspicuous consumption proclaiming the triumph of the French bourgeoisie. It takes honours as the world's largest theatre, though it seats only 2,000 people.

The **grands boulevards** leading from the Opéra to the Madeleine are perhaps less fashionable than in their heyday at the turn of the century, but the bustle and the great open sweep of the street make it easy to recapture the atmosphere. On the Boulevard des Capucines you will be retracing the footsteps of Renoir, Manet and Pissarro, who took their paintings to the house of photographer Nadar, at number 35, for the first exhibition of Impressionistic painting in 1874. The boulevards are now appropriately the home of the town's most popular cinemas—appropriately because it was here at the Hôtel Scribe, that the Lumière brothers staged the first public moving-picture show in 1895, causing queues around the block that have never disappeared in this film-obsessed city.

Many people are surprised to learn that the **Madeleine** is a church—and, in fact, it did not start out as one. Originally there *was* going to be a church here, and Louis XV even laid its first stone in 1764, but the Revolution halted construction. Then Napoleon decided to put up a huge temple-like structure, Greek on the outside and Roman on the inside. It was variously projected as a stock exchange, the Bank of France, a theatre or a state banquet hall. Napoleon himself saw it as a Temple de la Gloire for his military victories until the architect persuaded him to build the Arc de Triomphe in-

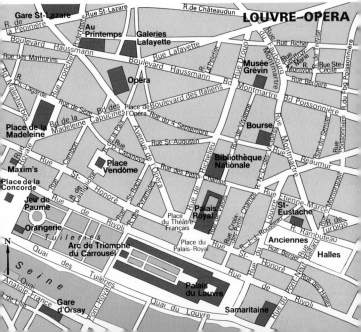

stead. After Waterloo Louis XVIII reverted to the plan for a church, but with no transept, aisles or bell-tower, or even a cross on the roof. It remains an awe-inspiring monument embellished on most days by the flower market at its base.

From the Madeleine you can either return to the Place de la Concorde by taking the grand Rue Royale past Maxim's restaurant, a monument no less awesome than the Madeleine, or go up towards the Etoile along the city's most opulent shopping street, the **Rue du Faubourg Saint-Honoré,** with a peek through the gates of the French president's Elysée Palace at number 55. But two other, entirely different neighbourhoods belong to and enrich the Right Bank: Montmartre and the Marais. Each deserves at least a day.

In Montmartre, the artist must also be adept at making a deal.

Montmartre

If Paris more than most places thrives on its mythology, few quarters have contributed more than Montmartre, known locally as "La Butte". Long famous as the home of artists and bohemian crazies, it is also a focus of the city's spiritual sources. The pagan and religious aspects of Montmartre's personality begin with the etymology of its name. Scholars still argue whether the popularly accepted derivation of Mons Martyrum, referring to the site of St. Denis's decapitation, is not a pious misconception of the true origins—Mons Mercuris, site of a pagan Roman temple.

A walk around Montmartre will help you make up your own mind. Still topographically the little country village of 400 years ago, it is impossible to drive a car around this area. Take the Métro, Porte de la Chapelle line, that goes from Concorde to Abbesses. (Do *not* get off at Pigalle; however attractive you may find its lurid glitter at night, by day it might depress you into not visiting the rest of Montmartre.)

From the Place des Abbesses, take Rue Ravignan to number 13, Place Emile-Goudeau. This was the site of the Bateau-Lavoir studio, an un-prepossessing glass-roofed loft that burned down in 1970. Here—if in any one place—modern art was born: Picasso, Braque and Juan Gris developed Cubism, while Modigliani worked his mysteries and Apollinaire sang it all in the first surrealistic verses.

Properly respectful of the spirits of the past, make your way around the neighbourhood where these "upstarts'" illustrious predecessors lived and worked—Renoir, Van Gogh, Gauguin, Utrillo—in the Rue Cortot, Rue de l'Abreuvoir, Rue Saint-Rustique (with the restaurant La Bonne Franquette where Van Gogh painted his famous *La Guinguette* now hanging in the Jeu de Paume museum). In artistic terms you move from the sublime to the ludicrous with the street-painters of the old **Place du Tertre.** Too rich a spot to be spoiled by the daubers, this is the very centre of Montmartre's village life, its original public square where marriages were announced, militiamen enlisted and criminals hanged. You should also visit the Rue Saint-Vincent, site of Paris' own vineyard, the Clos de Montmartre at the corner of the Rue des Saules, where they produce a wine that reputedly "makes you jump like a goat".

At the other end of Rue Saint-Vincent you come around the back of the basilica of **Sacré-Cœur.** You have probably spotted it a hundred times during the day so its back view will make a welcome change. This weird Romano-Byzantine church enjoys a dubious reputation in the city. The aesthetes quite simply hate its over-ornate exterior and extravagant interior mosaics, or at best find it grotesquely amusing; working-class people of the neighbourhood resent the way it was put up as a symbol of penitence for the insurrection of the 1871 Commune and defeat in the war against the Prussians. Sacré-Cœur's miraculously white façade derives from the special quality of the Château-Landon stone that whitens and hardens with age. For many its most attractive feature is the view from the dome, which can be visited, covering a radius of 30 miles on a clear day.

Just down the hill from the Sacré-Cœur is **Saint-Pierre-de-Montmartre,** one of Paris' oldest churches. Consecrated in 1147, 16 years before Saint-Germain-des-Prés, it repre-

Like an aging beauty's hair, the
38 *Sacré-Cœur grows daily whiter.*

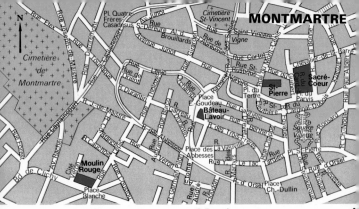

sents a significant work of early Gothic art, belied by its 18th-century façade. The Sacré-Cœur's architect, Paul Abadie, wanted to demolish Saint-Pierre, but he was overruled and a group of artists succeeded in having it restored, "as a worthy riposte to the Sacré-Cœur".

Every day's walk should end with a good rest and you should not be put off by the idea of going to the **Cimetière de Montmartre** off the Rue Caulaincourt, a place of delightful tranquillity often neglected for the more illustrious cemetery of Père-Lachaise (see p. 43). You can visit the tombs of Degas, Berlioz, Offenbach, Stendhal and Heinrich Heine and try to find the excellent bronze sculpture by François Rude at the grave of Godefroy Cavaignac.

Marais

The Marais district, north of the two river-islands, has bravely withstood the onslaught of real estate developers over the years, providing a remarkably authentic record of Paris' development from Henri IV at the end of the 16th century up to the Revolution. Built on land reclaimed from the swamps, as the name suggests, it contains some of Europe's most elegant Renaissance-style houses (*hôtels*), now serving as museums and libraries.

Start at the corner of Rue des Archives and **Rue des Francs-Bourgeois,** named after the poor people allowed to live there tax-free in 1334. (You take the Métro line Mairie des Lilas to Rambuteau.) The National Archives are kept here in a magnificent 18th-century mansion, **Hôtel de Soubise.** The beautiful horse-shoe-shaped *cour d'honneur* leads you into an exquisite rococo world: the apartments of the Prince and Princess of Soubise, the high point of Louis XV decor, contain the Musée de l'Histoire de France.

A garden (not always open to the public) connects the Soubise with its twin, the **Hôtel de Rohan** on Rue Vieille-du-Temple. Be sure to look for Robert Le Lorrain's magnificent stone sculpture, *Chevaux d'Apollon*, over the old stables in the second courtyard.

Two other architectural jewels grace the Rue des Francs-Bourgeois—the **Hôtel Lamoignon** at the corner of Rue Pavée and the **Hôtel Carnavalet,** once the home of the illustrious lady of letters Madame de Sévigné and now the Musée Historique de la Ville de Paris (see p. 71).

With a fine dramatic sense, the Rue des Francs-Bourgeois ends at what many consider to be the city's most picturesque square, **Place des Vosges.** Its classical harmony is achieved by a subtle diversity of detail in the gables, windows and archways of its red-brick façades. When Henri IV had the square built in 1605, on the site of a horse-market, it consisted of 36

homes or *pavillons*, each encompassing four arches, nine *pavillons* on each side. But these have since expanded or contracted according to the means of the owners. Place des Vosges remains one of the most luxurious residential areas of Paris. (Even if many of the façades were renovated by painting fake brickwork, the overall effect is still enchanting.) The gardens of the square, now a peaceful playground for children, were a favourite spot for the aristocratic duel and, after Louis XIII's wedding festivities here, the town's most fashionable promenade.

In those days it was known as the Place Royale. It received its current name for the prosaic reason that the department of the Vosges was the first to pay up all its taxes to the Revolutionary Government. If you are a fan of Victor Hugo, stop by the fascinating **museum** of his manuscripts, artefacts and 350 of his drawings at 6 Place des Vosges.

You can finish your visit to the Marais with a walk around the old **Jewish quarter.** Jews have lived continuously on the Rue des Rosiers since 1230, and Rue Ferdinand-Duval was known until 1900 as the Rue des Juifs. The other main street of the quarter, Rue des Ecouffes (a scavenger-bird that was a medieval slang-word for moneylender), remains a lively shopping quarter, with Jews

Henri IV made Place des Vosges a lovely place to live. It still is.

from North Africa gradually replacing the Ashkenazi of Poland and Hungary who themselves took over from the original Sephardim.

Père-Lachaise

Such is Paris' perpetual homage to the great of its past that the Cimetière Père-Lachaise manages to be an inspiring and quite undepressing pilgrimage for tourists and Parisians alike. This vast "City of the Dead" has a population estimated at 1,350,000 buried since its foundation in 1804. Named after Louis XIV's confessor, a member of the Jesuits who previously owned the

land, the cemetery has long been renowned as the resting place for the heroes of the country's revolutions. It even served as a battleground on May 28, 1871, for the last stand of the Communards and a "Mur des Fédérés" marks the place where they were executed by firing-squads at the southeast corner. In this pantheon of the city's artistic heritage, you will find writers Colette and Alfred de Musset and Italian composer Rossini at lot No. 4, Chopin (11), philosopher Auguste Comte (17), painters Ingres (23), Corot and Daumier (24), La Fontaine and Molière (25), Sarah Bernhardt (44), Balzac (48), Delacroix (49), Bizet (68), Proust (85), Apollinaire (86), Isadora Duncan (87), Oscar Wilde (89) (with a fine monument by sculptor Jacob Epstein) and Gertrude Stein (94). Napoleon's emancipation of the Jews meant that they could have their own section and Napoleon III's deference to the Turkish ambassador for his Eastern foreign policy led to an area for Moslems. Presidents of the Third Republic like Adolphe Thiers and Félix Faure lay just a stone's throw from the radicals they bitterly opposed. Père-Lachaise remains a unique site of national unity and reconciliation.

The Islands

Ile de la Cité

Shaped like a boat with the Square du Vert-Galant as its prow, the Ile de la Cité is the veritable cradle of the city of Paris, the original dwelling place of the fishermen and bargees of early Lutetia. The island also exemplifies what over-ambitious, wilful urban planning can do to charming neighbourhoods. In the middle of the 19th century, the much praised but often insensitive Baron Haussmann swept away nearly all of the medieval and 17th-century structures, leaving only the Place Dauphine and the Rue Chanoinesse (ancient home of the cathedral canons) as evidence of the island's rich residential life.

The baron was also thinking of replacing the triangular **Place Dauphine's** gracious red-brick, gabled and arcaded architecture with a neo-Grecian colonnaded square. But, fortunately, he was forced out of

In Paris' old quartiers, a bike is often the best way to get around.

office for juggling his books before the wreckers could move in. The *place*, close by the lively Pont-Neuf bridge, was built in 1607 by Henri IV in honour of his son the *dauphin* (later Louis XIII). Sadly only the houses at number 14 and 26 are still in their original state since 18th-century property developers found it more profitable to remodel the premises.

The massive **Palais de Justice,** today a complex of buildings encompassing the centralized legal machinery of modern France, holds echoes of the nation's earliest kings, who dwelt here, and of the later nobility, aristocracy and Revolutionary leaders, who were imprisoned here before execution. It also conceals a Gothic masterpiece, **La Sainte-Chapelle.** With its walls of stained-glass and its harmonious proportions (nearly equal height and length), the chapel has an ethereal quality—in startling counterpoint to the ponderous surrounding palace. It was built in 1248 by the pious King Louis IX (known as St. Louis) for the relics obtained from the emperor of Constantinople. There are in fact two chapels, the lower for the canons, chaplains and other dignitaries of the church, and the upper one for the king and his retinue.

The 15 **stained-glass windows** include 1,134 different pieces depicting mainly Old Testament scenes; 720 of them are 13th-century originals.

Between 1789 and 1815, the chapel served variously as a flour warehouse during the Revolution, a clubhouse for high-ranking dandies and finally as an archive for Napoleon's Consulate. It was this latter role that saved the chapel from projected destruction, because the bureaucrats did not know where else to put their mountains of paperwork.

These days they find space in the endless corridors of offices in the Palais de Justice and the nearby Préfecture de Police. What started off in 360 as the site of Julian's coronation as Emperor of Rome, later housing Merovingian kings Clovis, Childebert, Chilpéric and Dagobert, is now strictly "Maigret" country. The great Salle des Pas-Perdus is worth a visit for a glimpse of the lawyers, plaintiffs, witnesses, court-reporters and hangers-on waiting nervously for the wheels of French justice to grind into action.

But their anxiety is nothing compared with those who were condemned to bide their time in the prison of the **Conciergerie** (reached from the

Quai de l'Horloge). After April 6, 1793, when the Revolutionary Terror was in full swing, the Conciergerie (named after the royally appointed *concierge* in charge of common-law criminals) truly became the "antechamber of the guillotine". In the Galerie des Prisonniers, Marie-Antoinette, Robespierre, Saint-Just and Danton all spent their last nights after the Revolutionary tribunals had pronounced sentence. The Salle des Girondins displays one of the guillotine blades, the crucifix to which Marie-Antoinette prayed before execution and the lock from Robespierre's cell. Look out on the Cour des Femmes and see where husbands, lovers, wives and mistresses were allowed one last tryst before the tumbrels came. About 2,500 victims of the Revolutionary guillotine passed their final hours in the Conciergerie.

The site of the cathedral of **Notre-Dame de Paris** has had a religious significance for at least 2,000 years. In Roman times a temple to Jupiter stood here; some stone fragments of the early structure, unearthed in 1711, can be seen in the Cluny Museum (see p. 71). In the 4th century the first Christian church, Saint-Etienne, was built here, joined two centuries later by a second church, dedicated to Notre Dame. Norman invasions of Paris left the two edifices in a sorry state and the Bishop Maurice de Sully authorized construction of a cathedral to replace them in 1163. The main part of Notre Dame took 167 years to complete and the transition it represented from Romanesque to Gothic has been called a perfect expression of medieval architecture. One dissenting voice was that of St. Bernard, who protested that the godly virtue of poverty would be insulted by the erection of such a sumptuous structure. And some architectural purists today find Notre Dame a bit "too much". But it was built to inspire awe.

Old Baron Haussmann comes in for criticism again, because he greatly enlarged the *parvis*, or square, in front of the cathedral, thereby diminishing, it is said, the grandiose impact of the western façade. Others argue this brought back the animated street-life of the square, recapturing some of the gaiety of the Middle Ages when the *parvis* was used for public executions and the populace was invited to throw old fruit and rotten eggs provided by the authorities.

The cathedral remains an

impressive monument, truly the nation's parish church. It has witnessed, in 1239, Louis IX walking barefoot with his holy treasure, Christ's crown of thorns (before the Sainte-Chapelle was built); in 1430, the humiliation of having Henry VI of England crowned King of France; in 1594, Henri IV attending the mass which sealed his conversion to Catholicism and reinforced his hold on the French throne; in 1804, Napoleon's coronation as emperor, attended by the pope but climaxed by Napoleon crowning himself; and in our own day, the state funerals of military heroes such as Foch, Joffre, Leclerc and de Gaulle.

Given the cathedral's gigantic size, the balance of its proportions and the harmony of its façade are nothing short of miraculous. The superb central **rose window,** encircling the statue of the *Madonna and Child,* depicts the Redemption after the Fall. Look for the **Galeries des Rois** across the top of the three doorways. These 28 statues representing the kings of Judah and Israel were pulled down during the Revolution because they were thought to be the kings of France (later restored).

Inside, the marvellous lighting is due in large part to two more outsize rose windows dominating the transept. Don't miss the lovely 14th-century **Virgin and Child** that bears the cathedral's name, Notre-Dame de Paris, to the right of the choir entrance.

The original architect is anonymous but the renowned Pierre de Montreuil was

responsible for much of the 13th-century work. For the present structure with its majestic towers, spire and breathtaking flying-buttresses, we must be grateful to Eugène Viollet-le-Duc, who worked centimetre-by-centimetre over the whole edifice between 1845 and 1863, restoring the cathe-

Notre Dame cathedral, a national shrine of incomparable beauty, sits proudly on the island in the middle of the Seine where Paris was born.

dral after the ravages of the 18th century. For once, it was pre-Revolutionary meddlers—who tried to redecorate and improve—more than the Revolutionaries who where to blame. In 1831, Victor Hugo's novel, *Notre-Dame de Paris* started a public outcry that led to the restoration of the national shrine.

All the original bells have disappeared except for the *bourdon*, dating from 1400, in the South Tower. Its much admired purity of tone was achieved in the 1680s when the bronze bell was melted down and mixed with the gold and silver jewellery donated by Louis XIV's aristocracy. Today it is no longer operated by a hunchback but by an electric system installed in 1953.

Ile Saint-Louis

Very much a world apart, the Ile Saint-Louis is an enchanted, self-contained island of gracious living, long popular with Paris' affluent gentry. President Georges Pompidou lived here (on the Quai de Béthune) and loved to come here from the Elysée Palace as often as possible. The queen of French film actresses, Michèle Morgan, has an apartment on the corner of Rue Saint-Louis-en-l'Ile in the magnificent 17th-century mansion **Hôtel Lambert,** where Voltaire once enjoyed a tempestuous affair with the lady of the house, the Marquise du Châtelet.

Appropriate to the island's stylish reputation, its church, the **Saint-Louis-en-l'Ile,** is as elegant as one of its great mansions, bright and airy with a golden light illuminating a veritable museum of Dutch, Flemish and Italian 16th- and 17th-century art and some splendid tapestries from the 12th century.

The most striking of the mansions, the **Hôtel Lauzun** at 17 Quai d'Anjou, was built in the 1650s by the great architect Louis Le Vau, who also worked on the Lambert, the Seine façade of the Louvre and above all Versailles. The Lauzun's opulently ornamental decor was to provide a perfect setting for the Club des Hachischins frequented by Théophile Gautier and Charles Baudelaire.

But perhaps the island's greatest pleasure consists in walking along the poplar-shaded streets to the western end of Quai d'Orléans. There you have the most magnificent **view** of the apse of Notre Dame, which incorrigible romantics much prefer to the cathedral's "front".

Left Bank
(Rive Gauche)

Latin Quarter

To get an idea of what the Left Bank is all about, start at the Quartier Latin. Here, facing Notre Dame, the spirit of inquiry has traditionally been nurtured into protest and outright revolt before subsiding into a lifelong scepticism, as the rebels graduate from the university and move west to the more genteel Faubourg Saint-Germain. Starting in the 13th century, when the city's first "university" moved from the cloisters of Notre Dame to the Left Bank, the young came to the *quartier* to learn Latin.

In those days *l'université* meant merely a collection of people—students who met on a street corner, in a public square or a courtyard to hear a teacher, standing on a bench or at an upstairs window or balcony, lecture them. Today there are classrooms, overcrowded, but the tradition of open-air discussion continues, often over an endlessly nursed coffee or glass of wine at a café terrace on the Boulevard Saint-Michel or in the streets around the faculty buildings, or in the ever-present cinema queues.

52 Begin at the **Place Saint-**

Michel, where the Paris students come to buy their textbooks and stationery but the young of other countries come to sniff the Latin Quarter's mystique around the bombastic 1860s fountain by Davioud. Plunge into the narrow streets of the Saint-Séverin quarter—to the east Rue

Saint-Séverin, Rue de la Harpe, Rue Galande—into a medieval world updated by the varied exotica of Tunisian pastry shops, smoky Greek barbecue and stuffy little cinemas. A moment's meditation in the exquisite 13th–15th-century Gothic-Flamboyant church of Saint-Séverin, where Dante is

Advocating a Left Bank revolution doesn't rule out getting a suntan.

said to have prayed, and you are ready to confront the Latin Quarter's citadel, the **Sorbonne.**

Founded in 1254 as a college for poor theological students by

Robert de Sorbon, Louis IX's chaplain, the university was taken in hand by Cardinal Richelieu, who financed its reconstruction (1624–42). The Sorbonne's church houses the cardinal's tomb, and a memorial service is held for him every December 4 on the anniversary of his death. Visit the Grand Amphithéâtre, which seats 2,700, with its statues of Sorbon, Richelieu, Descartes, Pascal and Lavoisier, the great chemist. As you look at Puvis de Chavannes' monumental painting covering the back wall, *Le Bois Sacré*—allegorising Poetry, Philosophy, History, Geology,

Physiology and the rest—try to imagine 4,000 students packed into that hall in May 1968, arguing whether to have the whole thing plastered over. The student revolt against overcrowding, antiquated teaching and bureaucracy and the very basis of the social system made the Sorbonne the focal point of the movement. When police invaded the sanctuary—which for centuries had guaranteed student immunity—the rebellion was on.

Around the corner, as a kind of didactic inspiration for the students on what hard work can achieve, stands the gigantic Neo-classic **Panthéon,** resting place of the nation's military, political and literary heroes. Originally designed as the church of Sainte-Geneviève for Louis XV (1755), it was secularized during the Revolution as a vast mausoleum with the inscription "To our great men, the Fatherland's gratitude". But the Revolutionaries had a hard time deciding who merited the honour. Mirabeau and then Marat were interred and subsequently expelled. Napoleon ended the controversy by turning the Panthéon back into a church. Throughout the 19th century it went back and forth between secular and consecrated status, according to the regime's political colour. Finally Victor Hugo's funeral in 1885, the biggest the capital had seen, settled the Panthéon's status as a secular mausoleum. Hugo was buried there, followed (retroactively) by Voltaire and Rousseau, and then by prime minister Léon Gambetta, socialist leader Jean Jaurès, Emile Zola, inventor of the blind-alphabet Louis Braille, President Raymond Poincaré and many others.

After which, take a break in the **Jardin du Luxembourg.** If you want to picnic in the park (not on the grass), make a detour first to the old street-market behind the Panthéon on the bustling Rue Mouffetard by the tiny Place de la Contrescarpe, old hunting-ground of Rabelais and his spiritual descendants. Despite their 17th-century origins, the Luxembourg Gardens avoid the rigid geometry of the Tuileries and Versailles. The horsechestnut, beech and plane trees, the orangery and ornamental pond, best viewed from the east terrace near the Place Edmond Rostand entrance, were a major in-

Life's problems seem less arduous in a café on Boulevard St-Michel.

spiration for the bucolic paintings of 18th-century master Antoine Watteau.

Montparnasse

Montparnasse is where they invented the Can Can in 1845, at the now defunct Grande Chaumière dancehall. In the twenties it took over from Montmartre as the stomping ground of Paris' artistic colony, or at least of its avantgarde. American expatriates like Hemingway, Gertrude Stein, F. Scott Fitzgerald, John Dos Passos and Theodore Dreiser also liked the freeliving atmosphere and greatly added to the mystique themselves. Today French as well as American tourists point out the places where the Lost Generation found themselves.

Other quarters are known for their palaces and churches; Montparnasse (named after a 17th-century gravel mound since removed) has cafés and bars for landmarks. The Closerie des Lilas, a centre for French Symbolist poets at the turn of the century, served as a meeting-place for Trotsky and Lenin before World War I and for Hemingway and his friends after the war; the Sélect, first all-night bar to open in Montparnasse, in 1925, quickly became a Henry Miller hang-out;

La Coupole, which came along two years later on a site planned for a music hall, offered an even more outlandish set of "acts" each night; breakfast was taken at the Dôme, next door, just for a change of air; the Rotonde, favoured by Picasso, André Derain, Maurice Vlaminck, Modigliani and

Max Jacob, is now a cinema, but all the others survive along the bustling **Boulevard de Montparnasse.**

The strength of Montparnasse's myth is such that habitués can pretend not to see the 58-floor Tour Maine-Montparnasse office-skyscraper by the railway station.

There's always something going on in relaxed Jardin du Luxembourg.

Saint-Germain-des-Prés

Saint-Germain-des-Prés is the literary quarter par excellence, home of the major publishing houses, the Académie Française, bookshops and literary cafés, but also a charming neighbourhood for round-the-clock people-watching. In the years following the Liberation it was known as headquarters for Jean-Paul Sartre and his existentialist acolytes, who were dressed, winter and summer, in black corduroy and long woollen scarves. Foreign students abroad would flock here in the 1950s hoping to see the master at work or at least at play. Failing that, there were always the nightclubs off the Boulevard Saint-Germain, where you could listen to "le jazz hot" and smoke your lungs out.

Today the discotheques have replaced the jazz-cellars and existentialism has had its day, if that is not a contradiction in terms. But the easy-going atmosphere of the outdoor cafés continues around the Place Saint-Germain-des-Prés. On the north side you'll find the Café Bonaparte, on the west the famous Aux Deux Magots. Both provide ring-side seats for the street-theatre of mimes, musicians and fire-eaters, who collect money in hats, and for the neighbourhood eccentrics who offer their show for nothing. The Café de Flore up the boulevard has remained more relentlessly "intellectual" in atmosphere, perhaps because of its intense, ideologically confusing history. It has successively been the home of the extreme right-wing Action Française group under Charles Maurras in 1899, the Surrealists of Apollinaire and André Salmon in 1914 (they liked to provoke brawls), and then Sartre's existentialists, a peaceful bunch who never got enough sleep to have the energy for fighting.

Saint-Germain also has its more formal monuments. The church of **Saint-Germain-des-Prés,** a mixture of Romanesque and Gothic styles restored last century, has a clock-tower dating back to about 1000. A 17th-century porch shelters 12th-century doorposts.

To the north of the square runs the Rue Bonaparte, past the prestigious **Ecole des Beaux-Arts.** Incorporated in its structure are fragments of medieval and Renaissance architecture and sculpture that

Saint-Germain hardware store is a veritable goldmine for all manner of off-beat kitchen gadgets.

make it a living museum. More recently, in May 1968, it turned into a poster-factory when taken over by the students.

On the Rue des Beaux-Arts is the hotel where Oscar Wilde died in 1900, under the assumed name of Melmoth. He used to complain about the "horrible magenta flowers" of the room's wallpaper, saying "one of us has to go"—and now both have. The hotel has redone Oscar's room in what they consider a more fitting style.

The august Palais de l'Institut de France, home of the **Académie Française,** is on the Quai de Conti by the Pont des Arts bridge. Designed by Louis Le Vau in 1668 to harmonize with the Louvre across the river, the Institut began as a school for the sons of provincial gentry, financed by a legacy of Cardinal Mazarin. In 1805 the building was turned over to the Institut, which is comprised of the Académie Française, the supreme arbiter of the French language founded by Richelieu in 1635, plus the Académie des Belles Lettres, Sciences, Beaux Arts and Sciences Morales et Politiques. The admission of a

Académie Française, prime show-place for intellectual pyrotechnics.

new member to the Académie Française, an honour more exclusive than a British peerage, is the occasion of a great ceremony. Guides to the Institut like to point out the east pavilion, site of the old 14th-century Tour de Nesle. They say that Queen Jeanne de Bourgogne used to watch from there for likely young lovers whom she summoned for the night and then had thrown into the Seine.

The **Palais-Bourbon,** seat of the National Assembly, provides a rather formidable riverside façade for the Left Bank's most stately district— the elegant Seventh Arrondissement with its 18th-century foreign embassies, ministries and noble residences *(hôtel particuliers)*. The Grecian columns facing the Pont de la Concorde were added under Napoleon and belie the more graceful character of the Palais-Bourbon as seen from its real entrance on the south side. Designed as a residence for a daughter of Louis XIV in 1722, this government building can be visited only on written request or as the guest of a deputy. If you do get in, look for the Delacroix paintings on the history of civilization in the library.

The Foreign Ministry next to the *palais,* better known as the **61**

Quai d'Orsay, is more distinguished for its diplomatic language than its architecture (non-descript Louis-Philippe).

If you are more interested in gracious living than supreme power, you will probably agree with those who feel it's better to be prime minister and live at the **Hôtel Matignon** than be president at the Elysée Palace. The prime minister's magnificent residence at 57 Rue de Varenne is just a short walk from the National Assembly. Its huge private park has a delightful music pavilion much favoured for secret strategy sessions. The same tranquil street, a veritable museum of 18th-century elegance, contains the Italian Embassy, known as the **Hôtel de La Rochefoucauld - Doudeauville** (No. 47), and the Rodin Museum (see p. 71) in the **Hôtel Biron,** No. 77, which served as the home of Rodin, of poet Rainer Maria Rilke and dancer Isadora Duncan.

Invalides–Tour Eiffel*

From the quiet intimacy of this area we return to the massively monumental with the **Hôtel des Invalides,** Louis XIV's first vision of grandeur before Versailles and the work of the same architect, Jules Hardouin-Mansart. Picking up an idea from Henri IV, Louis XIV founded the first national hospital for soldiers wounded in the service of their country. In Napoleon's hands it also became an army museum, another celebration of his victories, and still later the supreme celebration of Napoleon himself, when his body was brought back from the island of St. Helena for burial in the chapel.

The awesomely elaborate tomb, set directly under an open space in the Invalides' golden dome, bears Napoleon's body dressed in the green uniform of the Chasseurs de la Garde. It is encased in six coffins, Chinese-box-fashion one inside the other, the first of iron, the second mahogany, then two of lead, one of ebony and the outer one of oak. The monument of red porphyry from Finland rests on a pedestal of green granite from the Vosges. Twelve colossal statues of Victories by Pradier frame the tomb.

The church of **Saint-Louis-des-Invalides** is decorated with the flags taken by French armies in battle since Waterloo. At the entrance to the Invalides are two German Panther tanks captured by General Leclerc

   * See map on page 27.

in the Vosges. The main courtyard contains the 18 cannons of the *batterie triomphale*, including eight taken from Vienna, which Napoleon ordered fired on momentous occasions. These have included the birth of his son in 1811, the Armistice of 1918 and the funeral of Marshal Foch in 1929.

The military complex continues with the **Ecole Militaire** and the vast **Champ-de-Mars** where officers have trained and performed military exercises since the middle of the 18th century. In its heyday, 10,000 soldiers passed in review on this expansive parade ground. Horse-races were held here in the 1780s and five world's fairs between 1867 and 1937. In this century it has been a park for the Left Bank's most luxurious residences.

There are monuments and there is the **Eiffel Tower.** Some

The nation's military tradition is on view at the Invalides museum.

Romance

A bewitching conspiracy that began with the 15th-century poet François Villon and continued with Maurice Chevalier, Gene Kelly and Edith Piaf has made Paris the supreme city of romance. This is the town, they say, where broken hearts come to mend, where faltering marriages perk up and casual friendships grow brighter with the city's enchanted light. There are places ideally suited for a kiss, a poem, an engagement ring, or whatever other madness this town may drive you to.

As a matter of fact, the municipal administration of Paris is an open and unashamed accomplice to the realization of your romantic dreams. A special service (at 5 Avenue Ledru-Rollin, Préfecture de Paris—Section Eclairage) enables you to have the monument of your choice illuminated for 15 minutes or more after the usual switching-off time (around midnight). Thus you can make your arrangements, stand near the Eiffel Tower or Notre Dame at, say, one minute to 3 a.m., and sigh: "Wouldn't it be marvellous if this whole place would suddenly light up?" And then 'Bingo!' the monument of your choice is bathed in light. The stuff dreams are made of!

celebrate heroes, commemorate victories, honour kings or saints. The Eiffel Tower is a monument for its own sake, a proud gesture to the world, a witty structure that makes aesthetics irrelevant. Its construction for the World's Fair of 1889 was an astounding engineering achievement—15,000 pieces of metal joined together by 2,500,000 rivets, soaring 984 feet into the air on a base of only 1,400 square feet. At the time, it was the tallest structure in the world.

At its inauguration the lifts were not yet operating and Prime Minister Pierre-Emmanuel Tirard, aged 62, stopped at the first platform (187 feet high), leaving his Minister of Commerce to go all the way up to the top to present Gustave Eiffel with the Legion of Honour medal. The tower was slated for destruction in 1910 but nobody had the heart to go through with it.

The critics hated it. Guy de Maupassant signed a manifesto against "this vertiginously ridiculous tower," and Verlaine rerouted his journeys around Paris to avoid seeing it (difficult now, almost impos-

Skateboarding enthusiasts appear unimpressed by Eiffel's stature.

64

sible then). But today it has become so totally the symbol of Paris that to dislike the Eiffel Tower is to dislike Paris.

The first two platforms both have restaurants and snack-bars. From the top platform you can theoretically see about 40 miles on a pollution-free day. The best time for the **view** is one hour before sunset.

The Louvre has its own Métro stop. Some people wish it had a train to take them through the galleries.

Museums

The Louvre

Open 9.45 to 5.15; certain galleries (including Greek and Roman sculpture, French painting and the *Mona Lisa*) stay open until 8 p.m. Closed Tuesdays.

The Louvre is so huge that people are sometimes frightened of going in at all. But you do not have to be an art fanatic to realize that to come to Pa-

ris without setting foot inside this great and truly beautiful palace would be a crime. If you do it right, it can be an exhilarating pleasure. First of all, get up very early on a sunny day and walk around its gardens in the Place du Carrousel (see p. 31). Admire the sensual Maillol statuary and then sit on a bench to take in the sheer immensity of this home of France's kings and storehouse of a world's treasures. At the east end is the Old Louvre, the Cour Carrée,

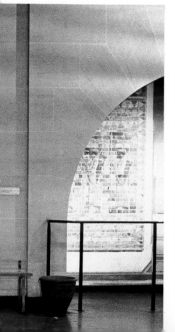

where Philippe Auguste built a fortress in 1190 to protect Paris from river-attack while he was away on a crusade. Stretching out from the Cour Carrée (of which you should see Perrault's marvellous colonnade on the east façade) are the additions of François Ier, Henri IV, Catherine de Médicis, Louis XIV, Napoleon and Napoleon III, nearly 700 years of construction.

François Ier, the Louvre's first art collector, acquired four Raphaels, three Leonardo da Vincis and one Titian (portrait of the king himself). By 1793 the palace possessed 650 works of art; at the last inventory, in 1933, there were 173,000. So do not be depressed if you don't see everything, but do try to take in the following (not arranged in order of preference):

1. **Victory of Samothrace.** A triumphant introduction to the collection, which you could not miss if you tried. This 200 B.C. Greek statue stands defiantly at the top of the Daru staircase by the main entrance. The right hand of the armless figure, found in 1950 near the original site of discovery, can be seen in a nearby glass case.

2. **Venus de Milo.** The proportions of this 2nd-century B.C. Aphrodite are perfect **67**

enough to stun the most world-weary cynic. Found by a peasant on the island of Melos in 1820 and snapped up by the French envoy to Istanbul, she now holds court in her own ground-floor room in the middle of the south side of the Cour Carrée.

3. **Michelangelo's** *Two Slaves*, a gift to Henri II in 1550, was intended for the tomb of Pope Julius II, the sculptor's protector. (In the Salle Michel-Ange on the ground floor of the Grande Galerie.)

4, 5 and 6. In the **Rembrandt Gallery** on the first floor, see especially *Self-Portrait with a Toque*, the artist as a young man, a cheerful one; *Hendrickje Stoffels*, a tender portrait of the companion of his later years and the healthy nude model for *Bathsheba Bathing*.

7. **Leonardo da Vinci's** *Mona Lisa (La Joconde)*, the most famous picture in the Louvre, if not the world, was bought by François Ier for 4,000 French *écus*. It took Leonardo four years to finish and he was never quite satisfied. The Louvre guardian who has watched over the *Mona Lisa* for the last 30 years said recently: "You know, some mornings she just doesn't smile." (In the Salle des Etats, signposted all the way.)

Louvre visitors debate merits of famous 16th-century French work.

8. **Titian's** *Woman at Her Toilet* is a delightfully voluptuous picture, arguably either of the Duke of Ferrara with his mistress or Titian himself with his (Salle des Etats).

9. **Poussin's** *The Arcadian Shepherds* is a gem of bittersweetness by France's greatest painter of the 17th century. (In the Fifth Section of Grande Galerie, whose décor he designed for Louis XIV.)

10. **Watteau's** *Embarkation for Cythera*—graceful, affectionate and tender. This is the perfect picture to encourage a Paris love-affair (Grande Galerie).

11. **Ghirlandaio's** *Old Man and His Grandson* juxtaposes in a charming manner the child's innocent wonder and the old man's ravaged sadness (Grande Galerie).

12. **Van Dyck's** *Charles I.* The English king's dignified grace makes you realize how difficult it must have been to chop his head off (Salle Van Dyck at west end of Grande Galerie).

13. **Rubens'** *Helena Forment* is a loving picture of his wife with two of their children (Salle Van Dyck).

14. **Jordaens'** *Four Evangelists* presents Matthew, Mark, Luke and John as men who have just done a hard day's work, very *Dutch* evangelists (Salle Van Dyck).

15. **Dürer's** *Self-Portrait* is a piercing, solemn portrait thought to have been a gift for his fiancée, Agnes Frey (Hol-

bein Cabinet north of Galerie Médicis).

16. **Velázquez's** *Queen Marianna of Austria.* The artist never seemed to worry about showing just how ugly these Habsburgs could be—and he still got work. (In the Spanish section at the end of the Grande Galerie.)

17. **El Greco's** *Christ on the Cross,* a powerfully mystic crucifixion, portrays a gaunt Christ in a tempestuous world (Grande Galerie).

18. **Ribera's** *The Club Foot.* The sheer good humour of this painting is a triumph of gruesome Spanish whimsy (Grande Galerie).

19. **David's** *Napoleon Crowning Josephine* in Notre Dame resembles a Hollywood-style extravaganza (Salle Mollien).

20. **Courbet's** *Funeral at Ornans* shows the French provincial bourgeoisie coming into its own, asserting its authority. In its day, the strong bleak realism of Courbet caused a great deal of consternation (Salle Daru).

Other Major Museums*

Though physically part of the Louvre, the **Musée des Arts Décoratifs** is a completely separate museum with its own entrance at 107 Rue de Rivoli. You should look out for the excellent temporary exhibitions devoted to great eras of design history and architecture, styles such as the Jugendstil, Bauhaus, and the American fifties. The permanent collection includes tapestries, lace, furniture, porcelain, and all aspects of domestic and institutional décor.

At the other end of the Tuileries Gardens on the Rue de Rivoli side is the **Jeu de Paume** museum of the Impressionists, a collection of the paintings that caused such an uproar in Paris in 1874. Some highlights: Edgar Degas's *Ballet Dancers* and *Café Concert;* Toulouse-Lautrec's *La Baraque de la Goulue;* Manet's famous *Déjeuner sur l'Herbe;* Van Gogh's portraits of *Docteur Gachet* and of himself; Cézanne's *Card Players* and *Apples and Oranges;* and others by Gauguin, Renoir and Monet.

On the river-side of the Tuileries, the **Orangerie** specializes in major retrospectives of 19th- and 20th-century artists. Regular visitors also love it for perhaps the most restful room in the city—the oval basement displaying the totally bewitching waterscape of Monet's *Nymphéas.*

The **Grand Palais** and **Petit Palais** (between the Champs-Elysées and the Seine) were both built for the World's Fair of 1900 and are now devoted to large-scale exhibitions of the great masters, though the Petit Palais does have some private collections donated to the

---

*Almost all museums close on
70   Tuesdays.

state, most notably, the Dutuit that includes paintings by Rubens, Teniers and Ruysdael and superb engravings by Rembrandt and Dürer.

The **Musée Guimet,** 6 Place d'Iéna, houses a magnificent collection of Oriental art from India, Indochina, Tibet, Indonesia, Japan and China.

At the **Musée de l'Homme,** devoted as the name implies to man himself, in the Palais de Chaillot, you can look upon the skull of Descartes, inside which the great thinker proved our existence.

The **Musée de Cluny,** 6 Place Paul-Painlevé in the Latin Quarter, is the best place to see the very beginnings of Paris as well as being the city's finest example of Gothic civic architecture. Within its grounds are the remains of the Roman public baths, the **Thermes de Cluny** dating from A.D. 200–300. You can still see the large arched room of the *frigidarium* or cold baths with a swimming pool on the north side, the *tepidarium* or luke-warm baths on the west side and the *caldarium* or steam room on the south-west side. Even older are the fragments of a monument to Jupiter (probably 1st century A.D.) found near Notre Dame cathedral. The fine Flamboyant chapel has an admirable Saint-Etienne tapestry, but the most celebrated tapestry in the museum is the world-renowned, 16th-century Boussac series, **The Lady with the Unicorn.**

The later history of Paris is charted in splendid detail at the **Hôtel Carnavalet** located at the corner of Rue des Francs-Bourgeois and Rue de Sévigné (closed on Mondays and Tuesdays). This elegant 16th-century mansion—a joy to visit for itself—has a fascinating collection of documents, engravings and paintings of the pomp, circumstance and drama of Paris' history. The outstanding exhibit devoted to the Revolution includes a letter from Robespierre dramatically stained with the author's blood: he was arrested and wounded while signing it.

There are also three delightful small museums devoted respectively to **Balzac** (47 Rue Raynouard), **Delacroix** (6 Rue de Furstenberg) and **Rodin** (77 Rue de Varenne), where you can see how these artists lived as well as admire their work. You'll find the *Thinker* and a bust of *Victor Hugo* in the garden of the Musée Rodin; the house contains the sculptor's private collection of Renoirs, Monets and Van Goghs.

Beaubourg

Open 10 a.m. to 10 p.m. on weekends, from noon on weekdays; closed on Tuesdays.

The government would have liked Paris' newest museum to be known by its official name: Le Centre National d'Art et de Culture Georges Pompidou or at least the Centre Pompidou (after the French president who sponsored it). But somehow since the Revolution, Parisians seem to have an aversion to naming their major monuments after their political leaders, and the 900,000,000-franc monster that is stirring up the same delight and rage as the Eiffel Tower will always be known quite simply as Beaubourg, after the 13th-century neighbourhood surrounding the centre.

This combination of public

Startling architecture of the Beaubourg serves as the backdrop for a year-round outdoor carnival.

library, modern art museum, children's workshop, *cinémathèque*, industrial design centre, experimental music laboratory and open-air circus aims to make culture readily accessible to the people. Six million visitors from all walks of life have responded to the challenge in its first year.

Beaubourg, designed by Italian Renzo Piano and Englishman Richard Rogers, looks a bit like an oil-refinery. The comparison is readily accepted by the architects, who deliberately left the building's service-systems visible and colour-coded: red for the transportation (elevators, escalators and freight-elevators), green for the water-pipes, blue for the air-conditioning ducts and yellow for the electrical system. The effect is undeniably startling and that in itself is stimulating in a Paris cultural climate that many feared was stagnating.

The plaza leading to the museum is an integral part of Beaubourg, thronged with crowds clustering around cowboys eating razor-blades, harlequins dancing and juggling, a peasant-philosopher examining a live chicken and egg for his dissertation over which came first. Beaubourg is a permanent festival.

The children have their own audio-visual centre. They are allowed to *touch* the outsize sculpture specially constructed for them and can even make **73**

their own. Composer Pierre Boulez is working with a group of avant-garde musicians at IRCAM (the Institut de Recherche et de Coordination Acoustique-Musique). In another workshop, ARTA (Atelier des Recherches Techniques Avancées) adults can play with computors. The modern art museum on the fourth and fifth floors, where the works are arranged chronologically, is ideal for the student.

But perhaps the great pleasure of Beaubourg is just going up it, in the long glass tubes that run diagonally from the bottom-left to the top-right-hand corner. Watch Paris unfold in front of your eyes with a rooftop **view**—best on the *fourth*, not the fifth floor—that many find much more satisfying than the Eiffel Tower view because you retain a sense of the city's dimensions.

Beaubourg has brought back an enthusiasm to Paris' cultural life that tourists may notice less than the residents. The big surprise about the statistics of the museum's visitors is that the overwhelming majority are *Parisians.*

Bois de Boulogne and Bois de Vincennes

To the east and west of the city, but incorporated now into its limits, are the two woods where Parisians take a breather. The **Bois de Boulogne,** more blithely known by residents of western parts of the city as *le Bois,* is the 2,224-acre remainder of the old Rouvray forest left completely wild until 1852. Napoleon III turned it into a place of recreation and relax-

Paris schoolchildren often make outings in the Bois de Boulogne.

ation for the people of Paris.

In the 17th century it was already a fashionable place, with aristocrats visiting the abbey at Longchamp (now the site of the race course) and building châteaux at La Muette and Bagatelle. Subsequently it was a favourite spot for duels and for people of dubious nocturnal habits. The transformations executed by Baron Haussmann, were among his happier achievements and the closest thing Paris has to a London-style park—with roads and paths for cycling and rambles, horse-trails, boating lakes, restaurants and cafés with open-air dancing. If you can, avoid Sundays, when legions of Parisians with their primly dressed children take possession of their prized playground.

One of the main attractions is the Parc de Bagatelle, a walled English garden with the city's most magnificent display of flowers.

Children enjoy the Jardin d'Acclimatation with its miniature train, Punch and Judy show, house of distorting mirrors, pony-rides and a miniature farm of pigs, goats and chickens.

The equally spacious **Bois de Vincennes** on the east offers much of the same attractions, plus France's largest zoo. This former royal hunting-ground has a more popular atmosphere than the Bois de Boulogne.

What to Do

Shopping

Shopping in Paris is a seductive, exotic adventure that turns adults into children and makes the children wish they had the adults' money. The choice of goods can be overwhelming and the attitude of salesmen and women sometimes forbidding, but if you go into the shop with a clear idea of what you

---

Paris Underground

One of the most fascinating tours offered by the municipality is through the **sewers.** In perfectly hygienic conditions you can take a guided boat tour underneath the streets (beginning by the Pont d'Alma), while the guide explains how the sewage has been chemically treated and distributed to fields outside Paris for the preparation of fertilizer—ever since 1868. In addition to the telegraph and telephone cables that take advantage of this intricate canalization, you can also see the unique *pneumatique* system of the post office, by which letters can be sent across Paris through compressed-air tubes like those used for passing change in old department-stores. Much favoured for love-letters and urgent demands for

unpaid rent, the letters reach their destination in a couple of hours.

Another weird underground attraction, for those with a taste for the spooky, is the **Catacombs** (entrance, 2 Place Denfert-Rochereau), a vast network of corridors scooped out under the city to provide building-materials above ground and a mass burial-place down below. The remains of 6 million unidentified dead lay here, transferred from overcrowded cemeteries across the city or buried here in times of mass deaths —like the Revolutionary Terror. Often the bones and skulls are laid out in gruesomely decorative arrangements. Over the entrance to this *ossuaire* are the words of poet Jacques Delille: "Stop, this is the Empire of Death".

want and a determined air, the aloof stares will melt into charming smiles. A cast-iron rule: never ask for what you want until you have said "Bonjour". (Don't worry if your French is not up to continuing the conversation beyond "Bonjour"; the new generation of sales people in Paris have a good command of English.)

The Big Stores

The department stores best equipped for dealing with foreigners are **Galeries Lafayette** and **Au Printemps,** next door to each other on the Boulevard Haussmann. Both have hostesses to help non-French-speaking customers, as well as the convenience of grouping selections from the major boutiques in their clothes departments. The Galeries has lost its great central staircase, but the circular galleries soaring above you still provide the most startling décor of Paris' big stores. They have an enormous chinaware department and excellent perfume and luggage sections. Au Printemps is famous for its lingerie and vast toy department.

For those who like the French habit of dressing up in baker's overalls, waiter's jackets, butcher's aprons, plumber's pants or sewer-worker's wad-ers, the **Samaritaine** department store at Pont-Neuf has an enormous selection of professional uniforms—52 different types representing 52 professions. It also offers a splendid view of the city from its 10th-floor bar.

FNAC, in the younger generation of Parisian department stores (at Châtelet, the Etoile and Montparnasse), has the city's largest selection of books and records, discounted 20 per cent.

A strange Parisian phenomenon is **Le Drugstore,** the Frenchman's conception of the American institution of an all-night pharmacy and soda-counter. In French hands it has become a go-go paradise of grocery-store, luxury gifts, news-stand, records, books, perfume, electronic gadgets, expensive luggage, car-rental, theatre-agency—and even a pharmacy—open till 2 a.m. (in Saint-Germain-des-Prés, near the Opéra, on Avenue Matignon and the Champs-Elysées). Americans scarcely recognize it.

Fashion

Paris wouldn't even bother to dispute the title of fashion capital of the world with London, New York or Rome. It would just send you to Rue du

Faubourg Saint-Honoré and Avenue Montaigne to see the masters of *haute couture:* Balmain, Lanvin, Cardin, Yves Saint-Laurent, Ungaro, Dior, Louis Feraud, Courrèges and Givenchy (on Avenue George-V), to name just a few. Most designers also have boutiques selling ready-to-wear clothing and accessories. The prices may be astronomical but the workmanship is still unequalled. Even if you cannot afford the prices, window-shopping can be as delightful as gallery-hopping— and give you ideas on what to look for in the cheaper shops.

At the second level in price and workmanship, but by no means lagging in creativity, are the chic little boutiques that have sprung up around Saint-Germain, Les Halles (the former food market) and on the Place des Victoires. These appeal especially to the young and slim or to those who want to look that way.

For leatherware, Hermès (Rue du Faubourg Saint-Honoré) is an institution all on its own, catering for the well-heeled horse-man, globetrotter and man-and-woman-about-town, with high-quality luggage, saddles, stirrups and boots and a much sought-after address-book.

Paris seems to make a great appeal to one's vanity and even visitors get caught up with the desire to look a little better and celebrate with a Parisian hair-do. You can find hairdressing with great flair and style at Alexandre, Carita, Maniatis, Jean-Louis David and Jacques Dessange, most of them with branches on both sides of the river.

Shopping in Paris runs from the sublime to the discarded: you can pay 5,000 francs for a designer dress or 5 for a flea-market curio.

Old and Not-So-Old

Antique-hunting in Paris takes place on two levels—the high-priced shops grouped mainly in the 6th and 7th *arrondissements* on the Left Bank and the flea-markets around the city-limits. Antiques from ancient Egyptian and Chinese through pre-Columbian to Louis XV, Second Empire, Art Nouveau and Art Déco can be found in elegant or poky little shops between the Quai Voltaire and Boulevard Saint-Germain, on the Rue Bonaparte, Rue des Saints-Pères, Rue de Beaune and Rue du Bac as you walk away from the river and then zig-zag the cross-streets of Rue de Lille, de Verneuil, de l'Université and Jacob. You will also find splendid collections of dolls and old toy-soldiers that cost a veritable military budget to buy.

The week-end **flea markets** are a well-established Parisian institution. The biggest, the Marché aux Puces de Saint-Ouen at the Porte de Clignancourt, in fact groups half-a-dozen markets. Vernaison specializes in musical instruments, lead-soldiers, old toys, buttons, brass and tinware; Biron has mostly antiques, not differing greatly in price from the Left Bank antique shops; Malik is a great favourite with the young for its Belle Epoque dresses, First World War military uniforms, 1920s hats, and an amazing assortment of Americana; Paul Bert might have that undiscovered masterpiece every flea marketeer dreams of—but get there early, practically at dawn, before the professional antique dealers begin rummaging among the unloading trucks; Jules Vallès is the smallest and cosiest, especially good for Art Nouveau lamps, some authentic military souveners, theatre costumes and old dolls.

The **bouquinistes** (second-hand booksellers) along the Seine—principally from the Place Saint-Michel to the Pont des Arts—are better now for old periodicals than for old books, with a strange nostalgia in the latter for the period of the German Occupation. If you are looking for old books on Paris itself, your best bet is Francis Dasté, Rue de Tournon. For the homesick, a good selection English and American books can be found at Galignani and W.H. Smith on the Rue de Rivoli and at Brentano's on the Avenue de l'Opéra.

Gourmet Shops

Paris, more than most cities, is a place from which to take **food** home as a souvenir. Mo-

For a whiff of the country, drop by the Ile de la Cité's flower market.

dern packaging makes it easier to transport goods that previously spoiled en route and many stores are equipped to export your purchases for you. The most famous luxury grocery shop is Fauchon, Place de la Madeleine. Despite their aristocratic reputation, the service is friendly, courteous and multilingual. Salespeople only become annoyed if you suggest **81**

they might not have what you are looking for. Of equally high standard but less comprehensive is Hédiard, on the other side of the Place de la Madeleine, which some people prefer for its more intimate, almost 19th-century atmosphere. For the best *foie gras*, perfectly canned for transportation, and for marvellous, sausages, hams and other *charcuterie*, try Coesnon, Rue Dauphine.

You may also want to take home some **wine.** The best bargains are at the Nicolas chainstores—150 branches in Paris. The greatest selection is at Le Grand, Rue de la Banque (bankers and stock-brokers are notorious connoisseurs). The most intriguing wine-shop is perhaps Caves de la Madeleine, Cité Berryer (off the Rue Royale), where an Englishman holds wine-tasting sessions.

Finally there are the markets—all over town—but particularly colourful on the Rue Mouffetard, Maubert-Mutualité and Rue de Seine on the Left Bank and Rue des Martyrs and Passy on the Right Bank.

Man cannot live by bread alone— but a baguette *is more than bread.*

Sports

As the back-to-nature movement gains ground, hitherto blasé Parisians are increasing their interest in sports and *le jogging* or *le footing, le squash* and *le bowling* are winning new adherents. The Bois de Boulogne and de Vincennes are favourite spots for **joggers;** more challenging is the hilly Parc Montsouris. Others trot along the Seine on the non-highway stretches of the Left Bank between Pont-Neuf and Pont-Royal. **Cycling** has always been a great French sport and you can hire a bike at Rent-a-Bike, or Paris-Vélo, as it is also known, Rue du Fer-à-Moulin (see also p. 105).

You can play **tennis** on public courts by contacting the Fédération Française de Tennis (2 Av. Gordon-Bennett), or resorting to the jungle-law of first-come-first-served at the Luxembourg Gardens' six amazingly cheap public courts. There are also over 400 clubs to which some hotels have access for their guests.

Swimming is a pleasant joke at the Piscine Déligny, a freshwater pool on the Seine near the Palais-Bourbon, where sunbathers go in minimal costume. More serious action takes place at the Olympic-size indoor pool **83**

of the Centre de Natation, 34 Boulevard Carnot, or in one of the 30 other good municipal facilities.

To learn the bizarre art of **French boxing**—where men in long underwear use their feet as well as fists—sign on for a course at the Académie de Boxe Française, Rue Servan.

Skating is possible from September until May at the Palais

Last push to the finishing line of prestigious Tour de France race.

de Glace, Avenue Franklin Roosevelt; Patinoire Olympique, Rue du Commandant-Mouchotte; and Patinoire Molitor, Avenue de la Porte-Molitor.

In spectator sports, pride of place goes to **horse racing.** Longchamp and Auteuil in summer are every bit as elegant as Britain's Ascot. The serious punter who wants to avoid the frills and champagne can have a very good time at Vincennes at the trotting races. Betting also takes place in town at the Pari-Mutuel desks of the corner *café-tabac.*

Football and rugby can be seen at the modern flying-saucer-like stadium of Parc-des-Princes and tennis at Roland-Garros, both in the Bois de Boulogne. The great popular fête of the Tour de France cycling race ends in July with a colourful sprint up the Champs-Elysées.

Excursions

Any excursion outside Paris must include **Versailles** (21 km.), where Louis XIV created the most sumptuous royal court Europe had ever seen, partly for his own glory and partly to keep his nobles in impoverished dependency and away from the intrigues of that trouble-making city of Paris. Architects Louis Le Vau and Jules Hardouin-Mansart and landscape-designer André Le Nôtre began their huge undertaking in 1661. It was completed 21 years later. After the Revolutionary ravages, it became a historic museum in 1832 and was restored in this century.

One of the principal attractions of the château is the **Galerie des Glaces.** Here Wilhelm was proclaimed Kaiser of Germany in 1871, after his victorious war against the French, and the peace treaty of World War I was signed in 1919. The most impressive façade is in the west, facing the gardens. Try to be there at 5 p.m. when the fountains begin to play. You should also see the **Grand Trianon,** the little palace that Louis XIV used to get away from the château, the **Petit Trianon** that Louis XV preferred, and the **Hameau** or "cottages" where Marie-Antoinette went to get away from everything.

You might like to venture further afield to the magnificent Gothic cathedral at **Chartres** (95 km. from Paris), which has the finest stained-glass windows in France, or to the château at **Rambouillet** (54 km.), the summer residence of the French president, where heads of state get together to lament the price of petrol in the beautiful park. An hour's drive north of Paris is the lovely **Forêt de Compiègne** (76 km.), perfect for a cool walk and picnic. You can rent horses at the village of SAINT-JEAN-AUX-BOIS in the middle of the forest and visit the famous clearing in the north-east corner where the armistice was signed in a sleeping-car in 1918—the same sleeping-car that Hitler forced the French to use to sign their capitulation in 1940. A replica of it stands there with a little museum commemorating the events.

Other nearby sights include the early Gothic basilica of **Saint-Denis** (4 km. from Paris) with royal tombs from the Middle Ages and Renaissance, the national ceramic workshops and museum of **Sèvres** (12 km.), the elegant château and racing course of **Chantilly** (42 km.), **Senlis** (44 km.), where you will find yet another beautiful Gothic cathedral, and the famous forest and château of **Fontainebleau** (65 km.).

The château gardens at Versailles
are a miracle of French precision.

Entertainment

The Paris night-scene has lost none of the glitter and bounce that Toulouse-Lautrec made famous at the turn of the century. The myth he created in that Belle Époque has sustained itself over the years and visitors are surprised to discover that his Moulin Rouge, on Place Blanche, still puts on one of the great, boisterous **floor shows** of Europe. The rest of Pigalle is indeed sleazy, but it always was. Taste may have changed over the years but Pigalle has always managed to plumb its lower depths with a certain glee that continues to hold an almost anthropological fascination for visitors. Bright exceptions remain the Michou (Rue des Martyrs), a witty cabaret of talented transvestite imitators, and two music-halls that launched the careers of Josephine Baker, Maurice Chevalier, Fernandel and Mistinguett—the Folies-Bergère (Rue Richer) and the Casino de Paris (Rue de Clichy). The other floor-show in the grand tradition of girls with feathers, balloons and little else takes place in the Lido over on the Champs-Elysées. But perhaps the most famous modern-day girl-show, conceived with great choreographic talent and de-

cors in which the girls are dressed only in cunning patterns of light, is in the Crazy Horse Saloon (Avenue George-V).

On the Left Bank there are two floor-shows that combine pretty girls and transvestites in a nonstop riot of pastiche, satire and surprisingly wholesome entertainment at the Alcazar (Rue Mazarine) and Paradis Latin (Rue Cardinal-Lemoine).

If you would rather do the dancing yourself, a plethora of **discotheques** awaits you—either massive New York-style or chic Parisian. And post-war smoky basement clubs devoted

You pay a bit more than the bare minimum to see showgirls of Paris.

to "le jazz hot", where the existentialists went to relax after a bout with Jean-Paul Sartre, remain—minus the philosophers—at the Bilboquet (Rue Saint-Benoît) and the Caveau de la Huchette (Rue de la Huchette) on the Left Bank and the Slow Club (Rue de Rivoli) on the Right.

Those seeking what is felt to be more serious fare will be pleased that the **Opéra** has made a great revival under director Rolf Liebermann with innovative productions that **89** have won the respect of the demanding German, Austrian and American critics who for years ignored Paris. The Orchestre de Paris has also improved its reputation since the advent of musical director Daniel Barenboim. It is worth going to the hall itself for tickets since agencies add at least 20 per cent to the price and cancellations are returned directly to the hall.

The classical **theatre** maintains its exacting standards for Molière, Racine and Corneille at the Comédie Française (Rue de Richelieu) and more international works at the Odéon on the Left Bank. Drawing-room comedies and the like find a happy long-running home in the theatres around the *grands boulevards*.

If you feel your French is up to it, visit the tiny *café-théâtres* at which you can sip a drink while watching *chansonniers* in satirical cabaret or an avant-garde play. They are centred around the Marais or Montparnasse. For all of these it is a good idea to consult the excellent weekly entertainment-guides, *Pariscop* and *l'Officiel du Spectacle*.

For many, Paris' most important artistic attraction is not the opera, concerts, theatre or cabaret but the **cinema.** On a typical week you will find over 250 different films playing in town, a record that cineasts claim unequalled elsewhere. Paris is a film-crazy town where directors and even screenplay writers achieve a celebrity equal to that of the stars. To enjoy Paris' cinematic riches you should learn: a) not to be intimidated by queues—there

An Opéra gala—one of the truly great moments of the Paris season.

are always queues and you nearly always get in; b) the ushers expect to be tipped, it is their only income—one franc minimum; c) not to be surprised by applause, even in the middle of the film—cinema is not just an art here, it is a spectator-sport; d) the one franc more for tickets on the Champs-Elysées is often for the air-conditioning; e) never overdress in the Latin Quarter.

Perhaps from an excess of civilization or sophistication,

Paris has for a long time not been a town to celebrate national or religious holidays in any grand style, but there are two days worth noting: **Bastille Day** (July 14) when you can still find a *bal populaire* in the Marais and working-class *arrondissements* (9th, 10th, 11th, 12th, 13th, 18th, 19th and 20th), usually around the firestation; and **Assumption Day** (August 15) when Paris is totally empty and a sudden quiet heaven.

Wining and Dining

There are some tourists who come to Paris without visiting a single museum or church and who would not dream of "wasting" their time shopping. And yet, they come away with tales of adventure, excitement, poetry and romance—and the feeling they know the city inside out. They have spent their time wining and dining and sleeping in between meals. The onslaught of fast-food and snack bars has not staled the infinite variety of Paris' restaurants, *bistrots* and cafés, at which anything from a gorgeous feast to a piquant regional sausage is served in the knowledge that eating and drinking are not just a means of satisfying hunger and thirst.

You can best enter into the spirit of this by devoting one, two or even all your evenings to the delights of good food. Go all the way: aperitif, hors d'œuvre, fish course, meat course, cheese, dessert, brandy and coffee. Back home, weddings and anniversaries may be your only occasion. Here, all you have to celebrate is the city itself. Not to dine well in Paris is not to have been there.*

A Primer for Novice Gourmets
Paris has everything except a cuisine of its own. Instead, you can sample food from almost every region of France. But before sitting down to eat, it's useful to have a few basic notions of French cuisine.

First things first. Forgoing the hors d'œuvre does not necessarily mean that the main course will be served more quickly. Besides, it's worth trying some of the simplest dishes that do work genuinely as appetizers: *crudités*—a plate of fresh raw vegetables, tomatoes, carrots, celery, cucumber; or just radishes by themselves, served with salt and butter; *charcuterie*—various kinds of sausage or other cold meats, notably the *rosette* sausage from Lyon, *rillettes* (like a soft pâté) and *jambon* from Bayonne or Dijon; or *potages* —rich vegetable soup, with a base of leek and potato, or perhaps a *bisque de homard* (lobster).

Fish comes fresh to Paris every day. The trout *(truite)* is delicious *au bleu* (poached ab-

The only thing that's better than a dozen oysters... is two dozen.

* For more about wining and dining in France, consult the Berlitz EUROPEAN MENU READER.

Handling the Waiter

Because French restaurants are regarded as secular temples, tourists sometimes feel they must treat waiters and maîtres d'hôtel like high priests and cardinals. First rule: never be in awe of them. They will not bite. If they bark, bark back. These people are not ogres by nature. They grow testy only when you show you are frightened or aggressive—much like the rest of us, really. You must remember that being a waiter is a respected profession in France, and they like nothing better than for you to call on their expertise.

If you are not satisfied with the wine or the meat is too rare, say so. If you do it with a smile, the waiter will be too surprised to argue. In any decent restaurant, surreptitious tipping to get a table when you have not made a reservation is rarely a good idea. But an extra tip (on top of the 15% in the bill) *after* the meal if you are pleased with your service will be greatly appreciated and get you good service if you return. Amazing how human Parisians can be.

solutely fresh), *meunière* (sautéed in butter) or *aux amandes* (sautéed with almonds). At their best, *quenelles de brochet* (dumplings of ground pike) are simply heavenly—light and airy. The sole and turbot take on a new meaning when served with a *sauce hollandaise*, that miraculous blend of egg-yolks, butter and lemon juice with which the Dutch have only the most nominal connection.

For your main dish, expect your meat to be less well-done than in most countries—extra-rare is *bleu*, rare, *saignant*, medium, *à point*, and well-done, *bien cuit* (and frowned upon). Steaks (*entrecôtes* or *tournedos*) are often served with a wine sauce (*marchand de vin* or *bordelaise*) or with shallots (*échalotes*).

General de Gaulle once asked how one could possibly govern a country with 400 different cheeses. Most of them are to be found in Paris and it would be a crime, in the mere name of your sacred diet, not to try at least the most famous of them—the blue *Roquefort*, the soft yellow-white, crusted *Camembert* or *Brie* (the crust of which you can safely remove without offending true connoisseurs), and the myriad of goat cheeses (*fromage de chèvre*).

Desserts are perhaps the most personal of choices at a

meal but you should not miss the chance of a *tarte Tatin* of hot caramelized apples, said to have been invented by mistake by a lady named Tatin who put her pie in the oven upside down. Or *profiteroles*, delicate ball-shaped éclairs filled with vanilla ice-cream and covered with hot chocolate sauce.

Regional Cuisine

With these pointers as a basic gastronomic "vocabulary", you can begin to try out the various regional cuisines to be found around the capital.

Burgundy, the historic cradle of French culinary art, is ideal for those with robust appetites. This wine-growing region produces the world's greatest beef stew, *bœuf bourguignon*, beef simmered in red wine for at least four hours with mushrooms, small white onions and chunks of bacon. Its Bresse poultry is considered France's finest, and the Charolais beef provides the tenderest of steaks. The freshwater fish benefits from another great sauce, Nantua, made with the stock of crayfish *(écrevisses)* and cream. And don't be afraid of the *escargots* (snails). Start with half a dozen and you may find the chewy texture and garlic butter sauce addictive.

Lyon—the gastronomic capital of France, renowned for the quality of its pork, wild game, vegetables and fruit. If you are adventurous, try one of the rich peasant dishes like *gras-double à la lyonnaise*, tripe with onions and vinegar, the famous *saucisson de Lyon* or a succulent chicken *à la crème*.

Bordeaux—the second great wine-growing region and also justly famous for its *bordelaise* sauce, made with white or red wine, shallots and beef marrow, served variously with *entrecôte* steaks, *cèpe* mushrooms or (why not?) lamprey eels *(lamproie)*. A surfeit of them may have killed a few medieval kings but the right amount never hurt anyone. The region's Pauillac lamb *à la persillade* (with parsley) is best eaten pink *(rose)*.

Provence—the home of garlic, olives, tomatoes and the country's most fragrant herbs. From the coast between Marseille and Toulon comes the celebrated *bouillabaisse*, a Mediterranean fish stew that might contain rascasse, chapon, saint-pierre, eel, red mullet, whiting, perch, spiny lobster, crabs and other shellfish, seasoned with garlic, olive oil, tomatoes, bay leaf, parsley, pepper and (not authentic without it) saffran. It is also the home of frog's legs, *cuisses de* *grenouille*, much easier to digest, with garlic, parsley and butter, than you might think.

Landes, Languedoc, Périgord—the south-west famous for *pâté de foie gras* (goose-liver pâté) and truffles, and for all the richness of the goose and duck, especially the *confit d'oie* or *confit de canard*, made by cooking the bird slowly in its own fat and then keeping it for days, weeks and even months in earthenware jars. This is the base of the *cassoulet* with haricot beans, pork, mutton, small sausages, or whatever, one of the heartiest cold-weather meals imaginable.

And all that is only a beginning. There is the *choucroute garnie* (sauerkraut with meat) of Alsace, the oysters, mussels, sea-urchins from Brittany, the *quiche* (bacon and egg pie) from Lorraine, the *tripes à la mode de Caen* from Normandy and on and on.

If a restaurant offers a *menu* (meaning a special fixed-price meal with appetizer, main course and dessert—not the *carte*, which lists all the establishment's dishes), you can usually save quite a bit by taking it. Look, too, for house wine *(vin ouvert)* served by the *quart* (quarter) and *demi* (half) litre, or bottled by the restaurant. It's always cheaper.

The Monuments

Some of Paris' restaurants are veritable institutions, as prestigious and monumental as the Louvre or Notre Dame—in fact, the Tour d'Argent is known to some as "Notre Dame's third tower", both for its breathtaking view of the cathedral and for the gourmets' religious fervour for its celestial duck dishes. Maxim's is a red-velvet fairyland for kings, Greek tycoons, princesses and opera divas. L'Archestrate is the high temple of the *nouvelle cuisine*, that inventive new style of cookery which may serve a lobster fricassée with fresh mint *(homard à la menthe fraîche)* or a salad of veal sweetbreads with raw mushrooms *(ris de veau aux cèpes)*.

And there are lower-priced institutions like Lipp, home of writers, publishers and politicians; La Coupole, a massive hang-out for everyone from actresses and painters to bankers and colonels; and the Closerie des Lilas, bar-cum-restaurant for Montparnasse artists and intellectuals, haunted by the ghosts of Hemingway and Trotsky.

Good food, good wine and good company—that's Paris for you!

Wine

What is for many people the most intimidating of experiences—ordering a French wine—has in fact far fewer rules than you think. If you happen to like red wine more than white, you can safely and acceptably order red with fish; a light Beaujolais, Morgon or Brouilly chilled goes with both fish and meat. And if you prefer white, you can drink dry Burgundy with fish and Alsatian wine with everything, with impunity. Remember, in a Paris restaurant *you* are king. You prefer beer? Go ahead, it goes especially well with Toulouse sausage and Alsatian *choucroute*.

But if you do want a few basic pointers about the classic wines, the Burgundy reds divide easily into two categories, those that can more safely be drunk relatively young—the supple *Côte de Beaune* wines of *Aloxe-Corton*, *Pommard* and *Volnay*—and those that need to

age a little, the full-bodied *Côte de Nuits* wines of *Vougeot, Gevrey-Chambertin* and *Chambolle-Musigny*. The great Burgundy whites include *Meursault* and *Puligny-Montrachet*.

Bordeaux wines have four main regional divisions: *Médoc*, aromatic, mellow red with a slight edge to it; *Graves*, a soft, easy-to-drink red, both dry and vigorous like the Burgundies; *Saint-Emilion*, dark strong and full-bodied; and the pale golden *Sauternes*, sweet and fragrant, the most distinctive of the soft, aromatic whites. The lesser Bordeaux can all be drunk a couple of years old but good ones need five years.

The Loire Valley produces fine dry white wines, such as *Vouvray* and *Sancerre*, and robust reds like *Bourgueil* and *Chinon*. Perhaps the best-known red wine outside Bordeaux and Burgundy is the *Châteauneuf-du-Pape*, produced in the Rhone Valley and truly magnificent when mature. Other very drinkable regional wines include *Côtes du Rhône, Cahors* and the *Riesling, Traminer* and *Sylvaner* of Alsace.

And for a sparkling finish, the nation's pride and joy, from that little area east of Paris between Reims and Epernay: *Champagne*, which they describe as *aimable, fin et élégant*, "friendly, refined and elegant".

A votre santé!

To Help You Order...

Do you have a table?
Do you have a set-price menu?

Avez-vous une table?
Avez-vous un menu à prix fixe?

I'd like a/an/some...

J'aimerais...

beer	**une bière**	menu	**la carte**
butter	**du beurre**	milk	**du lait**
bread	**du pain**	mineral water	**de l'eau minérale**
cheese	**du fromage**		
coffee	**un café**	potatoes	**des pommes de terre**
dessert	**un dessert**		
egg	**un œuf**	salad	**une salade**
fish	**du poisson**	sandwich	**un sandwich**
glass	**un verre**	soup	**de la soupe**
ice-cream	**une glace**	sugar	**du sucre**
lemon	**du citron**	tea	**du thé**
meat	**de la viande**	wine	**du vin**

... and Read the Menu

agneau	lamb
ail	garlic
anchois	anchovy
andouillette	tripe sausage
artichaut	artichoke
asperges	asparagus
aubergine	eggplant
bar	sea-bass
bifteck	steak
blanquette de veau	white veal stew
bœuf	beef
cabri	baby goat
caille	quail
canard, caneton	duck, duckling
cervelle	brains
champignons	mushrooms
chou	cabbage
chou-fleur	cauliflower
concombre	cucumber
côte, côtelette	chop, cutlet
courgettes	baby marrow (zucchini)
coquelet	baby chicken
coquilles Saint-Jacques	scallops
crevettes	shrimps
daurade	sea bream
écrevisse	crayfish
endive	chicory (endive)
épinards	spinach
flageolets	dried beans
foie	liver
fraises	strawberries
framboises	raspberries
frites	chips (French fries)
fruits de mer	seafood
gigot (d'agneau)	leg (of lamb)
haricots verts	green beans
homard	lobster
huîtres	oysters
jambon	ham
langouste	spiny lobster
langue	tongue
lapin	rabbit
loup de mer	sea-bass
macédoine de fruits	fruit salad
médaillon	tenderloin
moules	mussels
moutarde	mustard
mulet	grey mullet
navarin	lamb stew
nouilles	noodles
oignons	onions
oseille	sorrel
petits pois	peas
pintade	guinea fowl
poisson	fish
poire	pear
poireaux	leeks
pomme	apple
porc	pork
potage	soup
poulet	chicken
radis	radishes
raisins	grapes
ris de veau	sweetbreads
riz	rice
rognons	kidneys
rouget	red mullet
saucisse/ saucisson	sausage/dried sausage
saumon	salmon
sole	sole
sorbet	water-ice (sherbet)
thon	tunny (tuna)
truffes	truffles
veau	veal
volaille	poultry

How to Get There

From Great Britain and Eire

Most visitors from the U.K. travel to France individually, either by booking directly with a ferry operator and taking the car, or signing up for inclusive holidays which offer fly/drive and touring or self-catering arrangements.

BY AIR: Scheduled flights leave from London's Heathrow and Gatwick airports and also from Glasgow, Edinburgh, Manchester, Cardiff and several other British cities as well as Dublin, Ireland.

Charter Flights and Package Tours: Most tour operators charter seats on scheduled flights at a reduced price as part of a package deal which could include a weekend or a couple of weeks' stay, a simple bed and breakfast arrangement or a combined "wine tour" and visit to Paris. Among the inclusive holiday packages are special tours for visitors with a common interest such as cookery courses, school trips or art.

BY ROAD: Ferries or hovercraft services to Calais or Boulogne are recommended crossings for Paris. The toll motorway runs directly from Calais to Paris. A quieter country road, with the same mileage, leads from Boulogne to Paris.

BY RAIL: The journey from London takes from 7 to 11 hours by train. British and French Railways offer London-to-Paris service via Gatwick and Le Touquet or via Southend and Le Touquet with a possibility of overnight carriages from London.

BY BUS: Regular services go from London to Paris (via Calais) and from Manchester, Oldham and Rochdale (via Boulogne). The buses leave Victoria Station in London four times a week using the night crossing from Dover.

From North America

BY AIR: Daily non-stop flights go to Paris from more than a dozen major U.S. and Canadian cities. Many smaller cities have daily connecting flights to either of Paris' airports.

Although you can get to Paris in four hours from New York or Washington, D.C. on the Concorde, normal jet planes take about seven hours but cost a lot less. You can save by booking one of the following special fares:

The **APEX** (Advance Purchase Excursion) fare must be bought 30 to 45 days before departure and is valid for a stay of 14 to 45 days. You must pay a supplement for weekend flights. There are also seasonal variations in fares, the lowest being from October to April.

Excursion fares don't require advance reservations or payment and there are no cancellation fees. Two possibilities are the 14- to 21-day or the 22- to 45-day Excursion.

Budget fares for mid-week travel (Tuesday, Wednesday or Thursday only) are limited to certain flights. Tickets must be purchased when the reservation is made, and the passenger is subject to a "fine" in case of cancellation. Stays are from 14 to 45 days with fares slightly higher in peak season (June through August).

Youth fares for travellers between 12 and 23 are offered by most major carriers. There is no minimum stay, and the maximum is one year. Reservations cannot be confirmed until five days before departure.

Package Tours and Charters: ABC (Advance Booking Charters) provide air passage only (from New York, Chicago, Los Angeles and San Francisco to Paris), but OTC (One Stop Inclusive Tour Charter) package deals include airport transfers, hotel, some sightseeing and meals.

Paris is the starting point for many tours of France. Wine tasting, gourmet and cooking tours, as well as tours of the château country are included in package deals leaving from over a dozen major American and Canadian cities, usually on a seasonal basis (April to October) and for periods of from one to three weeks. You can also choose from fly/drive and fly/rail schemes.

BY SEA: You can book passage on the *Queen Elizabeth II* either to or from Europe, with part of the price including the air fare in the other direction. Certain sailings stop at Cherbourg with free air transfers from there to Paris.

From Australia, New Zealand and South Africa

Australia: There are two direct flights from Sydney every week for Paris and several other flights during the week which require a change in the Far East. Package deals for Paris are offered by certain airlines, and excursion fares are also available. The European Excursion fare to Paris requires a minimum 21-day stay (six-month maximum); APEX fares, paid 60 days before departure, require a minimum 14-day stay (maximum 45 days). Special fares are available for university students.

New Zealand: Flights leave daily from Auckland on regularly scheduled airlines. Package deals can be obtained which include accommodation, sightseeing and transport. Excursion fares for minimum 21-day stays and with two night stop-overs in each direction (in either Los Angeles, San Francisco, Hong Kong or Singapore) are offered.

South Africa: Besides scheduled flights from Johannesburg there are excursions from either Johannesburg or Cape Town and numerous package deals including Paris among other European sights.

When to Go

Paris enjoys a mild Continental climate without extremes of hot and cold. From mid-July to the end of August there seem to be more foreign than French people in Paris and shopkeepers and restaurant owners often close up and go on holiday themselves. The best seasons to visit Paris are spring and autumn. The following chart gives an idea of the average monthly temperature in Paris:

	J	F	M	A	M	J	J	A	S	O	N	D
°C	3	4	7	10	14	16	19	18	15	11	6	4
°F	37	39	45	50	57	61	66	64	59	52	43	39

Planning Your Budget

To give you an idea of what to expect, here's a list of average prices. They must be regarded as approximate, however, and inflation is running at around 10 per cent annually.

Airports: by bus: 13 F; by train: 10 F; by taxi: 60–100 F.

Babysitters: 9–12 F per hour.

Bicycle and Moped Rental: bicycle: 90–140 F per week (deposit 200–300 F); moped: 40 F a day (deposit 400 F).

Car Hire: *Renault 5:* 50 F a day, 0.50 F per km, 850 F weekly unlimited mileage; *Simca 1307:* 60 F a day, 0.65 F per km, 1050 F weekly unlimited mileage; *Peugeot 504:* 70 F a day, 0.70 F per km, 1140 F weekly unlimited mileage. Third-party insurance usually included, 17.6 per cent tax extra; full coverage 12–15 F extra per day. Holders of major credit cards normally exempt from deposit.

Cigarettes: French: 3 F; foreign: 5 F; French cigars: 8–12 F for 20.

Food: Continental breakfast: 10–25 F, lunch or dinner (fairly good establishment): 50–90 F, coffee: 3–5 F, beer: 3–5 F, wine (bottle): 15 F and up, cocktail: 15–20 F, cognac: 10–15 F, whisky: 10–15 F.

Fuel: super: 2.65 F per litre; oil: 16 F per litre.

Guides and Interpreters: 200 F, for half-day (2–6 people); chauffeur-guide: 290 F half-day for two.

Hairdressers': man's cut: 15–40 F; woman's cut: 20 F and up; shampoo and set: 20–40 F; blow-dry: 30–45 F; colour rinse/dye: 30–50 F.

Hotels (double room w/bath): ******** L 300–700 F; ******** 200–500 F; ******* 130–300 F; ****** 80–150 F; ***** 50–100 F.

Laundry and Dry Cleaning: laundry: shirt: 4–6 F; blouse: 6–8 F; dry cleaning: jacket: 12–14 F; trousers: 10–12 F; dress: 20–35 F.

Métro: 2nd-class ticket: 2 F; 10 tickets *(carnet)*: 12.50 F 2nd class, 19 F 1st class; *carte orange:* 57 F 2nd class; tourist tickets (bus or 1st class Métro): 4 days: 33 F; 7 days: 55 F.

Nightclubs/discotheques: 25–60 F (admission and first drink). Cinema: 15–20 F.

Sightseeing: boats: 10 F; museums: 5 F (free or reduced on Sundays). Reductions for students and older people.

Taxis: starts at 5.50 F (at stations and terminals 1 F extra); 3–4 km trip: 13–16 F.

BLUEPRINT for a Perfect Trip

An A-Z Summary of Practical Information and Facts

> Listed after most main entries is an appropriate French translation, usually in the singular. You'll find this vocabulary useful when asking for information or assistance.

A

ACCOMMODATION—see **HOTELS**

AIRPORTS *(aéroport).* Paris is served by two main airports, the new Roissy-Charles-de-Gaulle, about 15 miles north of the city, and Orly, about 9 miles to the south-east, with its two buildings, Orly-Sud and Orly-Ouest. Most intercontinental flights use Charles-de-Gaulle, a space-age modular construction. Both airports have currency-exchange banks, excellent restaurants, snack bars, post offices and well-stocked duty-free shops.

There is regular and comfortable bus service between airports and between the airports and Paris. The buses leave every 15–20 minutes from about 6.00 a.m. to 11.00 p.m. There's service outside of those hours from the terminals in Paris to the airport 45 minutes before airport check-in time. The terminal *(aérogare)* for Charles-de-Gaulle airport is at Porte Maillot, near the Etoile. Orly is served by the Invalides terminal. Average time to the airports from these terminals is around 40 minutes; it takes an hour and a quarter to get from one airport to the other by bus. You should plan to leave early if you travel during peak traffic hours.

You can also reach the airports by rail at a very modest price. Trains leave every 15 minutes from 5.30 a.m. to 11 p.m. and take 30 minutes from the Gare du Nord to Charles-de-Gaulle. From Quai d'Orsay, Saint-Michel or Austerlitz stations to Orly the trip takes about 40 minutes. Trains leave frequently from early morning to late at night. See p. 103 for rates.

Le Bourget, Paris' oldest airport (with all amenities), is now used almost exclusively for charter flights. Buses run between the airport and the Invalides terminal.

Where's the bus/train for…? **D'où part le bus/le train pour…?**

BANKS and CURRENCY-EXCHANGE OFFICES *(banque; bureau de change)*. Hours vary, but most Paris banks are open from 9 a.m. to 4.30 p.m., Mondays to Fridays. A few banks and currency-exchange offices operate later and on weekends. The Paris Tourist Information Office can provide a list of these.

Your hotel will usually change currency or traveller's cheques into francs, but the rate is not favourable. Always take your passport when you change money.

I want to change some pounds/ dollars. **Je voudrais changer des livres sterling/dollars.**

BARBERS'—see HAIRDRESSERS'

BICYCLE AND MOPED RENTAL *(location de bicyclettes/vélomoteurs)*. Several agencies rent bicycles, mopeds and motorcycles for those intrepid enough to brave Paris traffic. Outside Paris (in Chantilly, for example) you can rent bicycles at the railway station. The only station in Paris which rents bikes is the Porte Maillot-Neuilly station, tel. 285 88 00, ext. 224. See also p. 103.

BUS SERVICE *(autobus)*. Bus transport around Paris and the suburbs is efficient, though not always fast. Stops are marked by red and yellow signs, with bus numbers posted. Buses generally run from 6 a.m. to around 9 p.m., some later. Service is reduced on Sundays and holidays. You use one, two or three tickets depending on the distance. You can buy a ticket as you board the bus; but for frequent bus travel it's less expensive to use one or two tickets from a series *(carnet)* purchased in Métro stations, special four- or seven-day tourist passes or the *carte orange* (see MÉTRO). Remember that bus and Métro tickets are interchangeable.

Does this bus go to…? **Est-ce que ce bus va à…?**
Do you go to…? **Est-ce que vous allez à…?**

C **CAMPING.** France is very well equipped in campsites *(camping)*; there are over 100 around Paris with good facilities. Details are available through the Touring-Club de France, 65, av. de la Grande-Armée, 75782 Paris Cedex 16 (tel. 502 14 00), the Fédération française de Camping et de Caravaning, 78, rue de Rivoli, 75004 Paris (tel. 272 84 08) and the Camping Club de France, 218, bd Saint-Germain, 75007 Paris (tel. 548 30 03).

CAR HIRE *(location de voitures).* All car-hire firms in Paris handle French-made cars and often foreign makes. Local firms sometimes offer lower prices than the big international companies, but you may have to turn the car in at the same place, rather than dropping it off in another town. See sample rates on p. 103.

To hire a car you must furnish a valid driving licence (held for at least one year) and your passport. Depending on the model you rent and the hiring firm, minimum age for renting a car varies from 21 to 25. Holders of major credit cards are normally exempt from advance deposit payments; otherwise you must pay a substantial (refundable) deposit for a car.

I'd like to hire a car tomorrow.	**Je voudrais louer une voiture demain.**
for one day/a week	**pour une journée/une semaine**
Please include full insurance.	**Avec assurance tous risques, s'il vous plaît.**

CHILDREN. The younger set will find a lot to do in Paris. The Eiffel Tower and boat trips are good fun for everyone. Paris' main zoo (open daily from 9 to 5.30) is in the Bois de Vincennes, easily reached by Métro. The Jardin d'Acclimatation of the Bois de Boulogne is a very special games-and-zoo park, complete with pony rides, marionette shows and other diversions. It may be quite costly, but children love it (open from 9.30 to 6.30 every day). There are also art workshops for kids on Wednesday and Saturday afternoons in the Centre Georges Pompidou, Plateau Beaubourg (tel. 277 12 33). Ask for the Atelier des Enfants.

Reputable student and service organizations can provide babysitters *(babysitter, garde d'enfant).* Ask at your hotel or the tourist office. You should try to request a sitter at least a day ahead. For prices, see p. 103.

If your child gets lost, don't worry; you'll surely be able to trace the wanderer at the local *commissariat*, or police station.

Can you get me a babysitter for tonight/tomorrow night?	**Pouvez-vous me trouver une baby-sitter pour ce soir/pour demain soir?**
I've lost my child.	**J'ai perdu mon enfant.**

CIGARETTES, CIGARS, TOBACCO *(cigarettes; cigares; tabac)*. Tobacco is a state monopoly in France, and the best place to buy your cigarettes is at an official *débit de tabac* (licensed tobacconist's). There are plenty of these—cafés, bars and many news-stands—bearing the conspicuous double red cone.

French cigarettes include brands with dark or light tobacco, with or without filter. Dozens of foreign brands are also available at higher prices (see p. 103).

A packet of…/A box of matches please.	**Un paquet de…/Une boîte d'allumettes, s'il vous plaît.**
filter-tipped	**avec filtre**
without filter	**sans filtre**
light tobacco	**du tabac blond**
dark tobacco	**du tabac brun**

CLOTHING *(habillement)*. The world's fashion capital is a varied show on the streets. Women feel at home in anything from classic suits to the latest zany mode or jeans. Discretion and practicality are the rule. Paris women don't dress up much in the evening, though you'll want a cocktail dress or dressy slacks and blouses for better restaurants, nightclubs and discothèques.

Some restaurants require jacket and tie for men; and you'll probably get better service at most hotels and restaurants in conservative dress.

Unpredictable continental weather requires a versatile wardrobe, though neither in summer or winter are you likely to meet extremes. For summer a good rule is lightweight clothing with a warm sweater or blazer and a raincoat. In winter, too, a raincoat is sometimes necessary, plus light woollen clothes and a warm coat and boots for the coldest days.

Will I need a jacket and tie?	**Dois-je porter un veston et une cravate?**

COMPLAINTS (*réclamation*)

Hotels and restaurants: Complaints should be referred to the owner or manager of the establishment in question. Try a firm attitude, and if this doesn't work you can take more serious steps. In the case of a hotel, you can consult the trade organization, the Syndicat Général de l'Industrie Hôtelière, 22, av. de la Grande-Armée, 75016 Paris; tel. 380 65 25 or 755 88 30. Serious complaints may also be taken to the Préfecture de Police de Paris, 7–9 bd du Palais, 75004 Paris; tel. 326 44 20, or 2, rue de la Cité, 75004 Paris, tel. 887 23 89.

Bad merchandise; car repairs: Within about 10 days of purchase a store will usually exchange faulty merchandise (if you have the receipt), but you will hardly ever get your money back. For complaints about cars or car repairs, members of automobile associations can consult the Touring Club de France, 65, av. de la Grande-Armée, tel. 502 14 00.

I'd like to make a complaint.　　　**J'ai une réclamation à faire.**

CONSULATES—see **EMBASSIES**

CONVERTER CHARTS. For fluid and distance measures, see p. 111–112. France uses the metric system.

Temperature

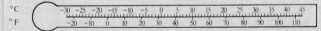

Length

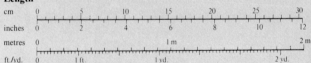

Weight

grams 0   100   200   300   400   500   600   700   800   900   1 kg
ounces 0   4   8   12   1 lb   20   24   28   2 lb.

CREDIT CARDS and TRAVELLER'S CHEQUES *(carte de crédit; chèque de voyage, traveller's cheque)*

Credit cards. Most hotels, smarter restaurants, some boutiques, carhire firms and tourist-related businesses accept certain credit cards.

Traveller's cheques. Hotels, travel agents and many shops accept them, although the exchange rate is invariably better at a bank. Don't forget to take your passport when going to cash a traveller's cheque.

Paying cash. Some shops or hotels may accept payment in sterling or dollars but the exchange rate will not be advantageous.

Do you accept traveller's cheques?	**Acceptez-vous les chèques de voyage?**
Can I pay with this credit card?	**Puis-je payer avec cette carte de crédit?**

CRIME and THEFT *(délit; vol).* Paris has its share of pickpockets, so watch your wallet and handbag, especially in crowds. Keep items of value in your hotel safe and obtain a receipt for them. It's a good idea to leave large amounts of money there as well.

Lock your car at all times and leave nothing valuable inside, or put what you're leaving in the locked boot(trunk). Any loss or theft should be reported at once to the nearest *commissariat de police* (see POLICE).

I want to report a theft.	**Je veux signaler un vol.**
My ticket/wallet/passport/handbag/credit card has been stolen.	**On a volé mon billet/portefeuille/passeport/sac à main/(ma) carte de crédit.**

CURRENCY *(monnaie).* For currency restrictions, see CUSTOMS CONTROLS. The French *franc* (abbreviated F or FF) is divided into 100 *centimes.* Current coins include 5-, 10-, 20- and 50-centime pieces as well as 1-, 5- and 10-franc pieces. Banknotes come in denominations of 10, 50, 100 and 500 francs.

Could you give me some (small) change?	**Pouvez-vous me donner de la (petite) monnaie?**

CUSTOMS CONTROLS *(douane).* Although there's no limit on the importation of foreign currencies or traveller's cheques, you may not leave the country with more than 5,000 French francs or the equivalent. So if you're travelling with more than this (in your own currency, traveller's cheques or other), you must fill out a declaration upon entry to enable you to re-export it later.

C The following chart shows what main items you may take into France duty-free:

Cigarettes	Cigars	Tobacco	Spirits	Wine
1) 400	100	500 g.	1 l.	2 l.
2) 300 or	75 or	400 g.	1½ l. and	3 l.
3) 200	50	250 g.	1 l.	2 l.

1) Visitors arriving from outside Europe
2) Visitors arriving from E.E.C. countries with non-duty-free items
3) Visitors arriving from E.E.C. countries with duty-free items, or non-E.E.C. European countries

For what you can bring back home ask before leaving home for the customs notice setting out allowances. See also ENTRY FORMALITIES.

| I've nothing to declare. | **Je n'ai rien à déclarer.** |
| It's for my own use. | **C'est pour mon usage personnel.** |

D **DRIVING IN FRANCE**

To take your car into France you will need:

International Driving Licence or your national driving licence	Car registration papers	Green Card (an extension of your regular insurance making it valid for foreign countries) or other third-party insurance valid for France
	Nationality plate or sticker	
	Red warning triangle	

Drivers and passengers of cars fitted with seat belts are required by law to wear them.

Driving regulations: As elsewhere on the Continent, drive on the right, overtake on the left, yield right-of-way to all vehicles coming from the right, even on roundabouts, unless otherwise indicated. Speed limits are 60 kph (kilometres per hour) in residential areas of Paris and its suburbs, 80 kph or 90 kph on through roads and 130 kph on motorways (expressways) called *autoroutes*.

Driving in Paris is hectic. Stick to your own pace and keep a safe distance between you and the vehicle in front. Be especially wary of vehicles coming from the right.

Road conditions: Beware of traffic jams on the major roads and motorways as you enter and leave Paris, especially on long weekends and around the summer dates of July 1 and 15, August 1 and 15 and September 1. Paris traffic police *(Gardiens de la Paix)* direct traffic and are helpful in giving directions (see POLICE).

Parking: This is a major problem in the capital, which authorities are trying to solve by building new underground parking lots, indicated by a large blue "P". In the centre most street parking is metered. The blue zones require the *disque de stationnement* (obtainable from petrol stations or stationers), which you set to show when you arrived and when you must leave.

Some streets have alternate parking on either side of the street according to which part of the month it is (the dates are marked on the signs). Fines for parking violations can be heavy, and in serious cases your car may be towed away or have a "Denver boot" attached (a metal tire lock that cannot be released) until you pay up at the local *commissariat*, or police station.

Breakdowns: Towing and on-the-spot repairs can be made by local garages, and spare parts are usually readily available for European cars. It's wise to have internationally valid breakdown insurance, and to ask for an estimate *before* undertaking repairs. Two companies which offer 24-hour breakdown service are Service Dépannage Automobiles, tel. 236 10 00 and SOS Dépannage, tel. 707 99 99.

Fuel and oil: Fuel is available in super (98 octane) and normal (90 octane). All grades of motor oils are on sale. Service-station attendants are tipped for any additional services rendered. See p. 103 for prices.

Fluid measures

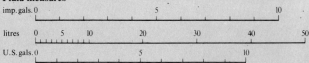

Distance

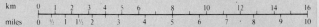

D **Road signs:** Most road signs are the standard pictographs used throughout Europe, but you may encounter these written signs as well:

Accotements non stabilisés	Soft shoulders
Chaussée déformée	Bad road surface
Déviation	Diversion (detour)
Douane	Customs
Gravillons	Loose gravel
Impasse	Cul-de-sac (dead-end)
Péage	Toll
Priorité à droite	Yield to traffic from right
Ralentir	Slow
Sauf riverains	Entry prohibited except for inhabitants of street
Sens unique	One-way street
Serrez à droite/gauche	Keep right/left
Sortie de camions	Lorry (truck) exit
Stationnement interdit	No parking
Véhicules lents	Slow vehicles

(international) driving licence	**permis de conduire (international)**
car registration papers	**carte grise**
Are we on the right road for…?	**Sommes-nous sur la route de…?**
Fill the tank, please.	**Le plein, s'il vous plaît.**
regular/super	**normale/super**
Check the oil/tires/battery.	**Veuillez contrôler l'huile/les pneus/la batterie.**
I've had a breakdown.	**Ma voiture est en panne.**
There's been an accident.	**Il y a eu un accident.**

DRY CLEANING—see **LAUNDRY**

E **ELECTRIC CURRENT.** You will probably only find 220-volt, 50-cycle A.C. in Paris although some of the oldest hotels may still have 110 volts. British and American visitors using electric appliances from home should remember to buy the necessary adaptors. For razors, just about all hotels have the possibility of both 110 and 220, or the razors themselves do.

EMBASSIES *(ambassade).* Contact your embassy or consulate when in trouble (loss of passport, theft or loss of all your money, problems with the police, serious accident).

Australia (consulate): 9, rue de la Fédération, 75015 Paris; tel. 575 62 00. Hours: 9 a.m.–12.45 p.m., 2–5.30 p.m., Mondays to Fridays.

Canada (consulate): 4, rue Ventadour, 75001 Paris; tel. 073 15 83 or 073 15 84. Hours: 9 a.m.–12.30 p.m. 1.30–5 p.m., Mondays to Fridays. Off-hour emergencies only (embassy): tel. 225 99 55.

Eire (consulate): 4, rue Rude, 75016 Paris; tel. 500 20 87. Hours: 10 a.m.–noon, 2–4 p.m., Mondays to Fridays.

New Zealand (embassy-chancellery): 7 ter, rue Leonard de Vinci, 75016 Paris; tel. 704 90 46. Hours: 9 a.m.–1 p.m., 2 p.m.–6 p.m., Mondays to Fridays.

South Africa (chancellery-consulate): 59, quai d'Orsay, 75007 Paris; tel. 555 92 37. Hours: 9.15 a.m.–noon, Mondays to Fridays.

United Kingdom (consulate): 109, rue du Faubourg Saint-Honoré, 75008 Paris; tel. 266 91 42. Hours: 9.30 a.m.–12.30 p.m., 2.30–5 p.m., Mondays to Fridays. Off-hour emergencies: telephone same number.

U.S.A. (embassy and consulate): 2, av. Gabriel, 75382 Paris Cedex 08; tel. 296 12 02 or 261 80 75. Hours: 9 a.m.–noon, 2–4 p.m., Mondays to Fridays. Call same numbers in off-hours.

Where's the… embassy/consulate?	**Où se trouve l'ambassade/ le consulat…?**
I'd like to phone the… embassy.	**Je voudrais téléphoner à l'ambassade…**
American/British Canadian/Irish	**américaine/britannique canadienne/irlandaise**

EMERGENCIES *(urgence)*. You can get assistance anywhere in France by dialling the number 17 for the police *(Police-Secours)*; 18 for the fire brigade *(pompiers)*, which also come for emergencies like gas asphyxiation and drowning. Paris has an efficient anti-poison centre (tel. 205 63 29). You can get advice for other urgent medical problems by dialling S.O.S. Médecins: 337 77 77. See also separate entries such as EMBASSIES, MEDICAL CARE and POLICE.

Careful!	**Attention!**	Police!	**Police!**
Fire!	**Au feu!**	Stop, thief!	**Au voleur!**
Help!	**Au secours!**		

Can you help me?	**Pouvez-vous m'aider?**

E **ENTRY FORMALITIES**. See also CUSTOMS CONTROLS and DRIVING IN FRANCE. Most visitors need only a valid passport—no visa—to enter France. British subjects can even enter on the simplified Visitor's Card. Though Europeans and North American residents are not subject to any health requirements, visitors from further afield may require a smallpox vaccination. Check with your travel agent before departure.

G **GUIDES AND INTERPRETERS** *(guide; interprète)*. The Agence Nationale pour l'Emploi, a public placement service, can usually find you a guide-interpreter at the lowest prices. Telephone 203 13 55 or 203 19 38. "Meet the French" (9, bd des Italiens; tel. 742 66 02/03/04) offers car with chauffeur-guide at a fixed price (excluding museum-entry tickets).

Reputable travel agencies also furnish guides and cars, and the larger hotels have lists of guide-chauffeurs. For prices see p. 103.

H **HAIRDRESSERS'** *(coiffeur)*. Prices vary widely according to the class of establishment, but rates are often displayed in the window.

Most *coiffeurs* include service charges in the price, but it's customary to give something. See p. 103 for prices.

Not too much off (here).	**Pas trop court (ici).**
Trim the fringe (bangs)/nape of the neck.	**Coupez un peu la frange/sur la nuque.**
I'd like a bouffant/smooth style.	**J'aimerais une coiffure bouffante/lisse.**

HEALTH *(santé)*. Fatigue, change of diet and over-indulgence (especially in wine) are the main culprits causing the common "tourist's complaint". Watch the drinking and try French mineral water, which helps to digest meals. Serious gastro-intestinal problems lasting more than a day or two should be looked after by a doctor. See MEDICAL CARE.

HOTELS and ACCOMMODATION *(hôtel; logement)*. Paris offers a wide range of hotels to suit every taste and budget. Advance bookings are highly recommended, since during holiday season and commercial exhibition weeks rooms can be almost impossible to find.

Officially, hotels are classified into five categories; a booklet is available at the Paris Tourist Information Office. Rates, fixed according to amenities and the hotel's location, should be posted visibly at reception desks and behind each room door. See page 103 for rates.

Newspapers such as *Figaro* and the *International Herald Tribune* list available accommodation for rent. Most houses and flats are available for long lease only, though some can be let for a month or less. Agencies take large fees, but some flats can be rented from the owner or subleased from the tenant without a fee.

See also CAMPING and YOUTH HOSTELS.

a double/single room	**une chambre à deux lits/un lit**
with/without bath/toilet	**avec/sans bains/toilettes**
What's the rate per night?	**Quel est le prix pour une nuit?**
I'm looking for a flat to rent	**Je cherche un appartement à**
for a month.	**louer pour un mois.**

HOURS *(heures d'ouverture)*. Although you'll find tobacconists' or small shops which sell food and wine open as early as 7 a.m. and as late as midnight, department stores and most shops do business from 9.30 a.m. to 6.30 p.m. Mondays through Saturdays. Boutiques and art galleries often stay open a bit later, especially in the summer. A few department stores are open until 10 p.m. on Wednesdays.

Watch out for variable lunch hours; businesses and smaller shops close for an hour or so. Banks and some offices close at noon on the day before public holidays. Most museums and monuments open around 10 a.m. and close about 5 p.m. Virtually all are closed on Tuesdays.

See also sections on POST OFFICE, BANKS AND CURRENCY EXCHANGE.

LANGUAGE. You'll usually hear well-enunciated French in Paris, spoken quite quickly. But there are myriad accents, since many Parisians come from the provinces, North Africa or further afield.

Although many Frenchmen speak some English, the French really appreciate a tourist making an effort to speak French, even if it's only the odd word.

The Berlitz phrase book FRENCH FOR TRAVELLERS covers almost all situations you're likely to encounter in your travels in France. In addition, the Berlitz French-English/English-French pocket dictionary contains an 8,000-word glossary of each language, plus a menureader supplement.

Good morning/Good afternoon	**Bonjour**
Good afternoon/Good evening	**Bonsoir**
Thank you	**Merci**
Please	**S'il vous plaît**
Goodbye	**Au revoir**

L You're welcome. **Je vous en prie.**
Speak slowly, please. **Doucement, s'il vous plaît.**
I didn't understand. **Je n'ai pas compris.**

LAUNDRY and DRY CLEANING *(blanchisserie; nettoyage à sec).* If your hotel will not take care of laundry or cleaning, you can have clothes cleaned quickly and cheaply in chain dry cleaners (not recommended, however, for fragile fabrics or difficult spots). Better care takes longer and is more expensive; prices vary according to fabric and cut. See p. 103 for sample rates.

When will it be ready? **Quand est-ce que ce sera prêt?**
I must have it tomorrow **Il me le faut pour demain matin.**
morning.

LOST PROPERTY *(objets trouvés).* If loss or suspected theft occurs in your hotel, check first at the desk. They may suggest you report the loss to the local police station *(commissariat).* Restaurant and café personnel are quite honest about returning objects left behind; they turn valuables over to the police.

Lost objects usually end up at the Bureau des Objets Trouvés, 36 rue des Morillons, 75015 Paris; tel. 531 82 10. Open Monday to Friday, 8.30 a.m.–5 p.m.; Thursday open until 8 p.m. If you've lost a passport, check first with your embassy, as the Bureau des Objets Trouvés would transfer it there first. Forms must be filled out in French, though there are usually English-speakers on hand.

I've lost my wallet/handbag/ **J'ai perdu mon portefeuille/sac/**
passport. **passeport.**

M **MAIL** *(courrier).* See also POST OFFICES. If you don't know ahead of time where you'll stay in Paris, you can have mail addressed to you c/o Poste Restante, 52, rue du Louvre, 75001 Paris, which is Paris' main post office.

The American Express at 11, rue Scribe, 75009 Paris, also holds mail. Take your passport with you to claim it.

Have you any mail for...? **Avez-vous du courrier pour...?**

MAPS. Small maps of the city *(plan)* are given away at tourist offices, banks and hotels. More detailed maps are sold in bookshops and at
news-stands. A good investment is the compact map book "Plan de

Paris" put out by A. Leconte. It contains a large fold-out map and small detailed ones of each *arrondissement*, with useful addresses. Falk-Verlag, Hamburg (the map producer for this book) also publishes a good map of Paris.

MEDICAL CARE. See also EMERGENCIES and HEALTH. To be at ease, make sure your health insurance policy covers any illness or accident while on holiday. If not, ask your insurance representative, automobile association or travel agent for details of special travel insurance.

Visitors from E.E.C. countries with corresponding health insurance facilities are entitled to medical and hospital treatment under the French social security system. Before leaving home, make sure you find out about necessary formalities and forms.

Paris has excellent doctors, surgeons and medical facilities. Most better hotels and the consulates have a list of English-speaking doctors and dentists. Doctors who belong to the French social security system *(médecins conventionnés)* charge the minimum.

Two private hospitals serve the Anglo-American community: American Hospital of Paris, 63, bd Victor-Hugo, 92202 Neuilly, tel. 747 53 00; British Hospital of Paris, 48, rue de Villiers, Levallois-Perret; tel. 757 24 10.

Chemists' *(pharmacies)* with green crosses are helpful in dealing with minor ailments or in finding a nurse *(infirmière)* if you need injections or other special care. The Pharmacie des Champs-Elysées, 84, av. des Champs-Elysées, tel. 256 02 41 is open 24 hours a day.

Where's the chemist on duty?	**Où est la pharmacie de garde?**
I need a doctor/dentist.	**Il me faut un médecin/dentiste.**
I've a pain here.	**J'ai mal ici.**
an upset stomach	**mal à l'estomac**
a fever	**de la fièvre**
headache	**mal à la tête**

MEETING PEOPLE. Cafés are a source of casual encounters and sometimes friendship, especially among the younger crowd in the Latin Quarter. You can also meet French people through a programme called Meet the French, a private organization (9, bd des Italiens, 75002 Paris; tel. 742 66 02/03/04) which proposes personalized guide service or even a meal with a French family in their home.

French people always kiss very close friends on both cheeks (sometimes more than once) and shake hands to greet or say goodbye to old and new friends and acquaintances.

M   Hello.   **Bonjour.**
        I'm glad to meet you.   **Enchanté.**
        How are you?   **Comment allez-vous?**

METRO. Paris' underground transport is possibly the world's most efficient, fastest and cleanest. It's also cheaper than most. New express lines (R.E.R.) get you into town in about 15 minutes, with a few stops in between.

You should buy a book of tickets *(carnet)*, available for first or second class, if you plan to take the Métro more than a few times.

For longer stays and lots of travel, you can buy an orange identity card *(carte orange)* valid for one month on buses and the Métro. There are also special tourist tickets for four or seven days, allowing unlimited travel on bus or first-class Métro. For prices see p. 103.

Big maps in every Métro station make the system easy to use. The service starts at 5.30 a.m. and ends around 1 a.m. See map on p. 128.

For 24-hour information on public transport in Paris phone 346 14 14.

Which line should I take for...?   **Quelle direction dois-je prendre pour...?**

N   **NEWSPAPERS and MAGAZINES** *(journal; revue)*. In addition to the local French dailies, you'll find the Paris-based *International Herald Tribune* almost everywhere and several English newspapers at many news-stands. Other local English-language publications are *The Paris Métro* (bi-weekly) and, quarterly, *A Touch of Paris. Pariscop* is the best known of the weekly information magazines on sale. A wide range of magazines in English and other languages is available at larger news-stands.

P   **PHOTOGRAPHY** *(photographie)*. Beautiful shots to be taken at so many street corners make Paris a photographer's dream. The city's hazy atmosphere and soft colours still inspire artists and photographers as they did the Impressionist painters.

All popular film makes and sizes are available; rapid development is possible, though sometimes expensive.

I'd like a film for this camera.   **J'aimerais un film pour cet appareil.**

a black-and-white film   **un film noir et blanc**
a film for colour prints   **un film couleurs**
118 a colour-slide film   **un film pour diapositives**

| How long will it take to develop this film? | **Combien de temps faut-il pour développer ce film?** | **P** |
| May I take a picture? | **Puis-je prendre une photo?** | |

POLICE *(police)*. In Paris you'll normally see the Police municipale wearing blue uniforms and *képi* hats. Also known as Gardiens de la Paix, they direct traffic, help tourists with directions, investigate violations and make arrests.

The C.R.S. police *(Compagnies républicaines de Sécurité)* are responsible to the Ministry of the Interior and often appear *en masse* around the French President's Elysée Palace (usually in dark-blue buses) during important political visits or when demonstrations take place.

The elegantly dressed *Garde républicaine*, often on horse-back and accompanied by a very good band, turn out for ceremonies and parades.

In case of need, you can dial 17 in Paris and all over France for police help.

| Where's the nearest police station? | **Où est le commissariat de police le plus proche?** |

POST OFFICE and TELEGRAMS *(poste; télégramme)*. See also MAIL and TELEPHONE. You can identify post offices by a sign with a stylized blue bird and the words Postes et Télécommunications *(P & T or PTT)*. Paris post offices are open from 8 a.m. to 7 p.m. Mondays to Fridays and 8 a.m. to noon on Saturdays. Stamps may also be bought at tobacconists'.

In addition to normal mail service, you can make local or long-distance telephone calls, send telegrams and receive or send money through the post office. The Paris Tourist Information Office has a list of post offices open on Sundays and holidays for telephone and telegraph services. You can send telegrams in English by telephoning 233 21 11.

Letters may be delivered within hours in the Paris district by sending them *pneumatique* from the post office. Another quick and even cheaper system for delivering a message is the *message téléphoné*. Inquire at the post office or your hotel.

| A stamp for this letter/postcard, please. | **Un timbre pour cette lettre/carte postale, s'il vous plaît.** |
| I want to send a telegram to... | **J'aimerais envoyer un télégramme à...** |

P   **PUBLIC HOLIDAYS** *(jour férié).* Following are the French national holidays. Remember that traffic is especially heavy on summer vacation dates. Public offices and banks, as well as shops, are closed on holidays, although you may find an occasional bakery or small food shop open.

January 1	*Jour de l'An*	New Year's Day
May 1	*Fête du Travail*	Labour Day
July 14	*Fête Nationale*	Bastille Day
August 15	*Assomption*	Assumption
November 1	*Toussaint*	All Saints' Day
November 11	*Anniversaire de l'Armistice*	Armistice Day
December 25	*Noël*	Christmas Day
Movable dates:	*Vendredi-Saint*	Good Friday
	Lundi de Pâques	Easter Monday
	Ascension	Ascension
	Lundi de Pentecôte	Whit Monday

Are you open tomorrow?   **Etes-vous ouvert demain?**

R   **RADIO and TV** *(radio; télévision).* There are three TV channels in Paris, all in colour. Programmes begin rather late in the day. Some hotels have television in the lounges, many in the top categories have sets in the rooms.

BBC programmes can be heard on short or medium-wave radios. In summer the French radio broadcasts news and information in English.

RELIGIOUS SERVICES *(offices religieux).* France is a predominantly Roman Catholic country. Mass *(la messe)* in English is said at St. Joseph's Roman Catholic Church, 50, av. Hoche; tel. 227 20 61.

There are three principal Anglo-American Protestant churches where services *(le culte)* are held in English:
The American Cathedral (Episcopal), 23, av. George-V; tel. 225 64 49.
The American Church (interdenominational), 65, quai d'Orsay; tel. 551 38 90.
St. Michael's Anglican Church, 5, rue d'Aguesseau; tel. 073 09 00.

The main synagogue in Paris is at 44, rue des Victoires; tel. 285 71 09.

What time is mass/the service?   **A quelle heure est la messe/ le culte?**

SUBWAY—see **METRO**

TAXIS *(taxi)*. You can find taxis cruising around or at the many stands all over town. You can also ring for radio-taxis, though they charge meter-fare for the trip to pick you up. For fares, see p. 103. You'll pay according to rates posted on the cab window, not just the price indicated on the meter (for example, extra charges for luggage).

TELEGRAMS—see **POST OFFICE**

TELEPHONE *(téléphone)*. International or long-distance calls are best made from your hotel or any post office. Local calls can be made from phone boxes or cafés. In a café you might have to buy a token *(jeton)* for the phone.

To get the overseas operator for a reverse-charge (collect) or person-to-person call you dial 19, wait for a second dial tone, then dial 33 followed by 11 for the U.S. and 44 for Great Britain. The operator can also tell you how to dial direct.

Can you get me this number in…?	**Pouvez-vous me donner ce numéro à…?**

TIME DIFFERENCES. France follows Greenwich Mean Time + 1, and in summer the clocks are put forward one hour. If your own time zone does likewise, the difference remains constant for most of the year.

New York	London	**Paris**	Sydney	Auckland
6 a.m.	11 a.m.	**noon**	9 p.m.	11 p.m.

What time is it?	**Quelle heure est-il?**

TOILETS *(toilettes)*. Paris is improving its public toilets, though sanitary standards are still far from perfect. Those near important Métro stops are generally modern and quite clean. Café W.C.'s are usually free, but you should order at least a coffee if you use the toilet. A saucer with small change on it means a tip is expected. If the toilet has

T no light-switch, the light will go on when you lock the door. The women's toilets may be marked *Dames*, the men's either *Messieurs* or *Hommes*.

Where are the toilets, please? **Où sont les toilettes, s'il vous plaît?**

TOURIST INFORMATION OFFICES (*office du tourisme*). Paris' main Tourist Information Office is extremely efficient: 127, Champs-Elysées, 75008 Paris; tel. 720 04 96. It is open every day in the tourist "season" (mid-March to October) from 9 a.m. until midnight. During the other months it's open until 10 p.m. They offer abundant documentation and a currency-exchange office. Other branches of the tourist office are located in major stations, airports and terminals, with varying opening hours.

RATP (Paris Transportation Authority) has tourist offices at 53 bis, quai des Grands-Augustins, Paris 6, and Place de la Madeleine, Paris 8. Some addresses of French tourist offices abroad:

Australia: French Government Tourist Office, Currency House, 23 Hunter Street, Sydney 2000, tel. 231 52 44.

Canada: 372 Bay Street, Suite 610, Toronto M5H 2W9, Ontario, tel. 361 16 05.

United Kingdom: 178 Piccadilly, London W1V 0AL, tel. 491 76 22.

U.S.A.: 610 Fifth Avenue, New York, N.Y. 10020, tel. 757-1125; 9401 Wilshire Blvd., Beverly Hills, Calif. 90212, tel. 272-2661, 271-6665; 645 North Michigan Avenue, Suite 430 Chicago, Ill. 60611, tel. 337-6301.

TRAINS (*train*). The French National Railways (*Société des Chemins de Fer Français* or S.N.C.F.) run excellent, punctual trains to all parts of France. They are linked to the European network.

The main stations in Paris are Gare du Nord (for British connections), Gare de l'Est, Gare d'Austerlitz, Gare Saint-Lazare and Gare de Lyon (for links with the Riviera, Spain and Italy). All types of accommodation are offered: first and second class, sleepers, the car-train (which combines the advantages of rail and car travel) and excellent restaurant service for longer trips.

Visitors from outside Europe should investigate the Eurailpass, a good way to travel unlimited miles within a certain length of time at a **122** flat rate. British visitors can procure a similar pass.

For routes and schedules inquire at the nearest tourist information office or the railway information counter.

When does the train for... leave?	**A quelle heure part le train pour...?**
single (one-way)	**aller simple**
return (round-trip)	**aller-retour**
first/second class	**première/deuxième classe**
I'd like to make seat reservations.	**J'aimerais réserver des places.**

TRAVELLER'S CHEQUES—see **CREDIT CARDS**

UNDERGROUND—see **METRO**

WATER *(eau)*. Tap water is safe in Paris and all over the country, except when marked *eau non potable* (unsafe for drinking). Several kinds of mineral water are sold everywhere. See also HEALTH.

a bottle of mineral water	**une bouteille d'eau minérale**
fizzy (carbonated)	**gazeuse**
still (non-carbonated)	**non gazeuse**
Is this drinking water?	**Est-ce de l'eau potable?**

YOUTH HOSTELS *(auberge de jeunesse)*. For visitors between 16 and 30, a pamphlet "Youth Welcome" lists more than 20 centres, accommodation and prices. Write to the tourist office asking for this list, then reserve in advance at the hostel of your choice.

Another useful address: Centre d'information et de documentation de la jeunesse, 101, quai Branly, 75015 Paris, tel. 566 40 20, open every day except Sunday.

SOME USEFUL EXPRESSIONS

yes/no	**oui/non**
please/thank you	**s'il vous plaît/merci**
excuse me	**excusez-moi**
you're welcome	**je vous en prie**
where/when/how	**où/quand/comment**
how long/how far	**combien de temps/à quelle distance**
yesterday/today/tomorrow	**hier/aujourd'hui/demain**
day/week/month/year	**jour/semaine/mois/année**
left/right	**gauche/droite**
up/down	**en haut/en bas**
good/bad	**bon/mauvais**
big/small	**grand/petit**
cheap/expensive	**bon marché/cher**
hot/cold	**chaud/froid**
old/new	**vieux/neuf**
open/closed	**ouvert/fermé**
Where are the toilets?	**Où sont les toilettes?**
Does anyone here speak English?	**Y a-t-il quelqu'un ici qui parle anglais?**
I don't understand.	**Je ne comprends pas.**
Please write it down.	**Veuillez bien me l'écrire.**
What does this mean?	**Que signifie ceci?**
Waiter/Waitress!	**Garçon/Mademoiselle!**
Help me, please.	**Aidez-moi, s'il vous plaît.**
Get a doctor—quickly!	**Un médecin, vite!**
What time is it?	**Quelle heure est-il?**
I'd like...	**J'aimerais...**
How much is that?	**C'est combien?**

DAYS OF THE WEEK

Sunday	**dimanche**	Thursday	**jeudi**
Monday	**lundi**	Friday	**vendredi**
Tuesday	**mardi**	Saturday	**samedi**
Wednesday	**mercredi**		

Index

An asterisk (*) next to a page number indicates a map reference.

METRO

A2 Boissy-St-Léger

13 St-Denis

A1 St-Germain en Laye

METRO STOPS
CONNECTING STATIONS
END-LINE STATIONS
RER CONNECTING STATIONS